THE DESERT

AMERICAN LAND CLASSICS

Charles E. Little
Series Editor

George F. Thompson
Series Director

American Land Classics makes available to a new generation of readers enduring works on geography, landscape, nature, and place.

Published in cooperation with the Center for American Places, Santa Fe, New Mexico, and Harrisonburg, Virginia

THE DESERT

FURTHER STUDIES IN NATURAL APPEARANCES

JOHN C. VAN DYKE

WITH A CRITICAL INTRODUCTION BY

PETER WILD

THE JOHNS HOPKINS UNIVERSITY PRESS
Baltimore and London

Introduction ©1999 The Johns Hopkins University Press
All rights reserved
Printed in the United States of America on acid-free paper
9 8 7 6 5 4 3 2 1

Originally published in a hardcover edition in 1901 by
Charles Scribner's Sons, New York
Johns Hopkins Paperbacks edition, 1999

The Johns Hopkins University Press
2715 North Charles Street
Baltimore, Maryland 21218-4363
www.press.jhu.edu

Frontispiece: John C. Van Dyke in 1898, at the time *The Desert* was
being written. Special Collections and Archives, Rutgers University
Libraries, New Brunswick, New Jersey.

Library of Congress Cataloging-in-Publication Data will be found at the
end of this book.
A catalog record for this book is available from the British Library.

ISBN 0-8018-6224-8 (pbk)

CONTENTS

CONTENTS

PREFACE-DEDICATION

To

A. M. C.

After the making of Eden came a serpent,
and after the gorgeous furnishing of the world,
a human being. Why the existence of the destroyers? What monstrous folly, think you,
ever led Nature to create her one great enemy
—man! Before his coming security may have
been; but how soon she learned the meaning of
fear when this new Œdipus of her brood was
brought forth! And how instinctively she
taught the fear of him to the rest of her children! To-day, after centuries of association,
every bird and beast and creeping thing—the
wolf in the forest, the antelope on the plain,
the wild fowl in the sedge—fly from his approach. They know his civilization means their
destruction. Even the grizzly, secure in the
chaparral of his mountain home, flinches as he
crosses the white man's trail. The boot mark

in the dust smells of blood and iron. The great annihilator has come and fear travels with him.

"Familiar facts," you will say. Yes; and not unfamiliar the knowledge that with the coming of civilization the grasses and the wild flowers perish, the forest falls and its place is taken by brambles, the mountains are blasted in the search for minerals, the plains are broken by the plow and the soil is gradually washed into the rivers. Last of all, when the forests have gone the rains cease falling, the streams dry up, the ground parches and yields no life, and the artificial desert—the desert made by the tramp of human feet—begins to show itself, Yes; everyone must have cast a backward glance and seen Nature's beauties beaten to ashes under the successive marches of civilization. The older portions of the earth show their desolation plainly enough, and the ascending smoke and dust of the ruin have even tainted the air and dimmed the sunlight.

Indeed, I am not speaking figuratively or extravagantly. We have often heard of "Sunny Italy" or the "clear light" of Egypt, but believe me there is no sunlight there compared with that which falls upon the upper peaks of

the Sierra Madre or the uninhabitable wastes of
the Colorado Desert. Pure sunlight requires for
its existence pure air, and the Old World has
little of it left. When you are in Rome again
and stand upon that hill where all good romanticists go at sunset, look out and notice how
dense is the atmosphere between you and St.
Peter's dome. That same thick air is all over
Europe, all around the Mediterranean, even
over in Mesopotamia and by the banks of the
Ganges. It has been breathed and burned and
battle-smoked for ten thousand years. Ride up
and over the high table-lands of Montana—one
can still ride there for days without seeing a
trace of humanity—and how clear and scentless,
how absolutely intangible that sky-blown sun-
shot atmosphere ! You breathe it without feeling it, you see through it a hundred miles and
the picture is not blurred by it.

It is just so with Nature's color. True
enough, there is much rich color at Venice, at
Cairo, at Constantinople. Its beauty need not
be denied ; and yet it is an artificial, a chemical
color, caused by the disintegration of matter—
the decay of stone, wood, and iron torn from
the neighboring mountains. It is Nature after
a poor fashion—Nature subordinated to the will

of man. Once more ride over the enchanted
mesas of Arizona at sunrise or at sunset, with
the ragged mountains of Mexico to the south of
you and the broken spurs of the great sierra
round about you ; and all the glory of the old
shall be as nothing to the gold and purple and
burning crimson of this new world.

You will not be surprised then if, in speaking
of desert, mesa and mountain I once more take
you far beyond the wire fence of civilization to
those places (unhappily few now) where the
trail is unbroken and the mountain peak un-
blazed. I was never over-fond of park and
garden nature-study. If we would know the
great truths we must seek them at the source.
The sandy wastes, the arid lands, the porphyry
mountain peaks may be thought profitless
places for pilgrimages ; but how often have you
and I, and that one we both loved so much,
found beauty in neglected marshes, in wintry
forests, and in barren hill-sides ! The love of
Nature is after all an acquired taste. One begins by admiring the Hudson-River landscape
and ends by loving the desolation of Sahara.
Just why or how the change would be difficult
to explain. You cannot always dissect a taste
or a passion. Nor can you pin Nature to a

board and chart her beauties with square and compasses. One can give his impression and but little more. Perhaps I can tell you something of what I have seen in these two years of wandering; but I shall never be able to tell you the grandeur of these mountains, nor the glory of color that wraps the burning sands at their feet. We shoot arrows at the sun in vain; yet still we shoot.

And so it is that my book is only an excuse for talking about the beautiful things in this desert world that stretches down the Pacific Coast, and across Arizona and Sonora. The desert has gone a-begging for a word of praise these many years. It never had a sacred poet; it has in me only a lover. But I trust that you, and the nature-loving public you represent, will accept this record of the Colorado and the Mojave as at least truthful. Given the facts perhaps the poet with his fancies will come hereafter.

JOHN C. VAN DYKE.

LA NORIA VERDE
FEBRUARY, 1901.

A CRITICAL INTRODUCTION TO
THE 1999 EDITION

A hundred years ago, a man strapped on a pistol, swung his leg over the back of his Indian pony, and, jaw set, rode off into the great, unknown spaces of the American desert. Bystanders clucked their tongues and gave knowing winks as he passed. Surely the man was daft, a fool. Everyone knew that those unmapped, trackless lands—those endless, waterless expanses of sand dunes, scorpions, and bandits—were oubliettes, the swallowing wastelands that made Southwestern deserts feared places. For that, they were called the Devil's Domain and the Lands That God Forgot. Simply put, men rode in there, but they rarely rode out again.

Over two years later, however, the fool in question, John C. Van Dyke, emerged from his trek through these dark lands. True, he was somewhat the worse for wear. Lost, sometimes crazed with thirst and loneliness, he had fought off bandits and a pack of wolves, and staggering delirious with thirst, he had slashed into cactuses to drink their life-sustaining liquid. However, all the torture was as nothing compared to the buoyancy of the discovery he had made. Those places were indeed infernal, Dantean in their horrors, testing to extremis the bravest man's mettle. But Van Dyke had found something else out there, something that his stay-at-home, naysaying detractors had never suspected. Those horrid lands of bare peaks in the fierce sun, of jumbled boulder fields stretching for miles unblessed by a blade of grass, for all their terrors, were beautiful places.[1]

Why, the very dunes, with sand finer than snow, curve and arch, sweeping over the landscape in lovely patterns "as graceful as the lines of running water" (*The Desert* 53). And those fearsome thunderstorms, whose sudden bursts were known to sweep away a man who was dying of thirst, also overwhelmed the lone traveler with appreciative awe as he beheld the boiling, rose-tinged clouds of nature's fury swell to fill the sky above him. Die of thirst? Yes, that always was a danger. But look at what one gained.

Sunsets anywhere around the world can be arresting, but none are so galvanizing as what one sees in the desert. Van Dyke rhapsodizes:

[1] Van Dyke gives this version of his desert travels in his *Autobiography* (117–25).

I have seen at sunset, looking north from Sonora some twenty miles, the whole tower-like shaft of Baboquivari change from blue to topaz and from topaz to glowing red in the course of half an hour. I do not mean edgings or rims or spots of these colors upon the peak, but the whole upper half of the mountain completely changed by them. The red color gave the peak the appearance of hot iron, and when it finally died out the dark dull hue that came after was like that of a clouded garnet. (91)

So the prophet declared, stepping from the wilderness. For out there, lashed those many months by nature—suffering from blackouts, depression, and Goodness knows what else—he had been writing, writing, back propped up against a rock, soaring with his pen above his tortures. Then he reentered civilization carrying the manuscript of the greatest book ever written about America's deserts. Van Dyke's message was clear: Not only are deserts the most beautiful places in the world, they are lands of freedom and adventure to America's bored and city-pent. For that, in his book Van Dyke saddled up again and, waving a generous hand, hailed his readers, stirring them from their lethargy and inviting them to ride off with him "far beyond the wire fence of civilization" into those trackless spaces of adventure, exhilaration, and spiritual renewal (xx).

As prophets go, Van Dyke was very lucky. Many

hailers of new "truths" are scorned for their radicalism—shunned, stoned, or worse—in any case, rejected by the larger society for their disturbing notions. As we shall see in more detail later, for complex reasons coming together at a pivotal point, Van Dyke's *The Desert* appeared at precisely the right time, when the public was ripe for its message. The book lifted the nation by its ears, and almost overnight, a utilitarian country all but unanimously grousing at deserts as God's mistakes, as noxious obstacles to civilization, turned about and saw those places with new eyes, in the lovely terms Van Dyke uses to describe them.

In evidence of this, published in 1901, when Van Dyke was in middle age, the little volume enjoyed an astounding longevity. Over the decades it went through reprint after reprint until Van Dyke's death, in 1932. And it is a longevity revivified. In our more recent, more ecologically tuned days, *The Desert* continues to be taught in courses in American literature and environmental studies. More dramatically, perhaps, its well-thumbed pages are borne along by countless backpackers, to be taken out in the evening, and chosen passages—a favorite being the sunset paean already quoted—chanted out over some stony abyss as the sun crashes down a final time, lending the dead rock incarnadined life before awed onlookers.

Although no one in the decades since the first publication of *The Desert* has come close to the power of Van Dyke's prose, part of the book's aura likely is the image that has grown up around the writer. Living in cities far more crowded, and certainly more beset by asphalt, than those inhabited by Van Dyke's original readers, we revel, if vicariously, on a guided tour through a land whose youth and pristine wonder we'll never know. And, perhaps more, we revel in the man who "saw it first and said it best" (Powell 327). In our age, so badly lacking in heroes, here is a man to meet our longings, an excellent blend—as we are not—of the two-fisted frontiersman and the fine-tuned male far ahead of his times in his sensitive feelings for the environment. Southwestern scholar Lawrence Clark Powell best reflects this. He describes the desert traveler as a fusion of the rugged outdoorsman with the intuitive "indoorsman," the writer with his delicate emotions pullulating on his sleeve (319). Also ably capturing Van Dyke's appeal, Richard Shelton, another student of the Southwest, paints a portrait of *The Desert*'s author as a man "in love with the desert. . . . He was in love, and the book is a by-product of that love affair" (Shelton xxvi–xxvii). In such ways, the volume, and the man behind it, glow in our memories. If John C. Van Dyke isn't a man for all times, he certainly is a man for *our* time, and, hence, the reissue of his little book as an *American Land Classic* to honor the volume's centennial at the millennium in 2001.

Newly compelling reasons, however, add to the further importance of this reissue. The two afore-mentioned professors deserve high praise for doing the spadework in modern studies of Van Dyke. There is a problem, however, in such happy scenarios applauded by Southwestern enthusiasts over the decades. As with other aspects of our lives, litera-ture sometimes is not what it seems to be. This surely holds true of Van Dyke's volume. Neither the man nor his much-praised book are what people popularly have imagined through a century of read-ing. To come to the nub of the issue: Van Dyke never took his famous trip, and his book is a grand fraud.

Far from being the Politically Correct desert saint whom the critics and public alike have enjoyed picturing over the decades, Van Dyke was a wealthy elitist from the East, allied with Andrew Carnegie, the richest and, some would say, the most nature-destroying man in America. Far from loving the wild land he so dramatically described, for Van Dyke it was a bauble, to be forgotten once he had his poetic way with it. And far from caring about the downtrodden urban masses he blithely invited to follow him into the wilderness, he not only despised his large audience, he ridiculed it for being so easily duped. And yet, for all that, there you have it, what remains the best book ever written about America's deserts.

At this point, lest the devotee of Van Dyke stomp off in a tiff at the betrayal, or the newcomer to this fine book throw it into the trash bin, I would like to rush in and say a number of things all at once. Yes, Van Dyke did see America's deserts, but he saw them while whizzing across the barren stretches in posh Pullman cars. Yes, too, his book, for all its factual errors, remains the loveliest work on the subject, which tells us something about the nature of at least some literature. Lastly, perhaps we are more culpable than he. How could a book—the really important questions are often the most painful—be reissued and applauded time after time for nearly a hundred years and not have one person—not a single naturalist, literary scholar, or just plain intelligent reader—challenge its obvious flaws in print?[2] This, in turn, leads us to suspect that *The Desert* tells

[2] The only possible exception I can think of is so gentle it might well be discounted. English art critic Peter Reyner Banham softly chided Van Dyke for "not always" understanding "the life forms he describes" (157).

us a great deal, not so much about the desert but about ourselves.

But not lastly, for one might turn the question inside out. Why would a man already famous for other books and, according to the best we can learn about his finances, hardly in need of money bother to write such a literary hornswoggler? And why would his buddies, those captains of industry and fellow artists, gathered in their salons among the riffle and flurry of servants and tinkling crystal, chuckle and wink at Jackie's little trick rather than condemn him for it? So you see that, fine reading that *The Desert* is, exploring the issues lurking behind its pages throws open doors on understanding not only ourselves but also the complexities of the milieu that gave birth to *The Desert*—and to its author. With Van Dyke, a man who reportedly could slay a woman with one intense glance of his dark eyes, we have a very foxy fellow indeed.

In pondering such things, our hearts leap, for ahead of us lies a rather strange, if not macabre, tour, not only to castles and the salons of the *haut monde*, but to a ruined hacienda deep in Mexico, to the most lavish private yacht of the day where Lillie Langtry and other beauties dally, and to an abandoned ranch on the Mojave Desert where, so locals will tell you, moaning ghosts still wander.

With such things in mind, we give thanks that past scholars were wrong and clap our hands that Van Dyke has finally broken the bonds of his image as the plaster saint of the desert. For this, he emerges as all the more fascinating a writer, and his famous book becomes far more intriguing than most readers have imagined through the decades.

To summarize the career of John C. Van Dyke is to get a peek into the unofficial aristocracy that once dominated much of America, for his birthplace, alone, sets the tone for much of his life. John was born in 1856 at Green Oaks, a three-peaked mansion rising among similar mansions of family members in the idyllic woodlands and rolling fields on the outskirts of New Brunswick, New Jersey. On the patronymic side, his ancestors stretch back in a distinguished Old Dutch line to the arrival of Thomasse Janse Van Dyke in New Amsterdam in 1652. His mother's family boasted a distinguished New England heritage, including his grandfather, a professor at Rutgers College (now University) and one of America's great mathematicians. Together, the two families could tick off the decades studded with Revolutionary War heroes, a famous spy, a famous poet, and any number of influential landowners and civic leaders.

However, as held true for many of America's aristocrats of the time, the Van Dykes were too comfortable with their laurels to bother much about dwelling on them. The Van Dykes were doers, not gloaters. John's father, also named John, was, at turns, an attorney, a bank president, a congressman, a friend of Abraham Lincoln, and a member of New Jersey's supreme court. Young John may have enjoyed a boyhood as idyllic as the countryside around him, hunting, fishing, and swimming in nearby Mile Run. Yet from those to whom much is given, much is required—a favorite Calvinist warning, likely much in his ears. Once, while tromping up the dark stairway to bed, young John yowled back to his elders reading below in the lamplight that there was a bear on the landing. Up from the living room floated the casual and quite practical advice: Well, then, "fight him off" (Van Dyke *Autobiography*, 33). In consequence, the five Van Dyke brothers took their fates in their hands and pursued professions, four, including John, becoming lawyers, one a medical doctor.

Yet, in the case of John, although he moved in the most select circles, the bear never went away. In the dark, often hidden side of his life lurked an ill-defined monster always happy to go another round with him. That is, John was wayward, an outlier, all his life torn between pride in his background and a search for new ways to prove his mettle. He was both aristocrat and rebel, neoteric and sentimentalist, and in that tension lay the seeds for his accomplishment.

In 1868, for reasons still not entirely clear, John's father moved the family to Minnesota. However, young John's heart yearned for the East. At the age of twenty-one, after attending Columbia Law School, he was admitted to the bar, but he never practiced. Instead, he plunged into the new currents of impressionistic art from Europe then frothing in New York City. He started to write art criticism. What was then considered Bohemian rebelliousness would serve him well. Writing books and articles for such culture bearers as *Century Magazine*, Van Dyke eventually became one of the best-known art critics in America. Back in hometown New Brunswick, he won the directorship of the library at the prestigious New Brunswick Theological Seminary and held a concurrent and equally prestigious position as the first professor of art history at Rutgers College. Thereafter, the pattern of Van Dyke's life was set. He throve on worldwide trips in search of art, but he always returned to idyllic, college-town New Brunswick, his tree-shaded refuge but a brief train ride from the excitements of New York City.

In the world of culture, Van Dyke had arrived. Book after book on art, nature, and travel were not all that marked his cachet. The rebel liked power. Advising Andrew Carnegie on which canvases to include in his growing collection, Van Dyke shot grouse and sipped tea with the lords and ladies visiting at Skibo, the steel magnate's sprawling castle on the Scottish moors. In line with this, Van Dyke was the familiar of Europe's great art museums, as completely at ease with the cultured summer throng in the courtyard of the Uffizi as he was in accepting the swift and silent service at the fashionable hotels lining the Champs Élysées. He appears—at least we're pretty sure he appears—riding the seas on the *Namouna*, the most sumptuous private yacht of the day. On this floating palace chockablock with late-Victorian beauties and wealthy gentlemen, he's taking a break from art, reading a book to a languorous Lillie Langtry.[3] In addition to this, he pops up in the strangest places, for instance,

[3] The issue is intriguing, but, as in so many other aspects of Van Dyke's life, we can't be completely sure. Van Dyke's comments in his *Autobiography* (150–51), as well as the oil *On the Yacht* Namouna, *Venice*, by painter of the fashionable Julius L. Stewart (reproduced in the photo section of the *Autobiography*, following 127), and my lengthy note 2 (243–44) in the same book assemble what light that, at this date, can be shed on the matter.

on a ranch in the middle of the Mojave Desert where he hobnobbed with John Muir and other visiting lights of the day. Another ranch and Van Dyke haunt, this one mentioned in a passing reference as a humble affair deep in Mexico populated by poor Indians, turns out to be an enormous hacienda, complete with its own chapel and a full complement of servants, the trysting place for Van Dyke's arrival with a bag of money.

Central to this often airy and sometimes mysterious life were Van Dyke's views of art. Along with many other adherents of Art for Art's Sake, Van Dyke looked on wild nature as the highest art, better than the canvases hanging in the world's great museums. Van Dyke, however, could be as hazy as any of his fellow enthusiasts in defining Art for Art's Sake, a gauzy offshoot of Romanticism. Basically, it came down to this: In counterbalance to the meaninglessness of life, one burned with Walter Pater's "hard, gem-like flame," thrilling that the recognition of beauty is life's highest good. Thus, "these wastes of sand" (*The Desert* 231) referred to earlier, so noxious to the pioneers who had stumbled through them, when seen by the fine-tuned observer speeding by in his Pullman car, needed no justification or meaning or use, except that "they are beautiful in themselves and good to look upon" (232). It was as if God, or the forces of the universe, or whatever one chose to believe in, had put lovely sand dunes there to be enjoyed at that moment by the passing traveler. One walks through life with his optic nerve pulsing with the joys of seeing—the problem being that Art for Art's Sake had no logical underpinnings. Each man knows what he likes, gleans his pleasure, and simply shrugs at anyone lowbrow enough to ask about logic or theory. As Van Dyke gestures in *The Desert*, all he can do is pass on his "impression" of what he sees (xxi). The why of it is not his worry.[4]

This is an enviable stance, unassailable in its lack of reasoned argument, and one can imagine a proponent such as Van Dyke enjoying his privileged status, his pockets full of money, breezing through his days from one wondrous beauty to another. It was not to be. If euphoric flights marked one of Van Dyke's poles, the opposite—for Freudian, neurological, or astral reasons I would not attempt to explain—was the Slough of Despair. Its results in the mercurial art critic were anger, spite, and bursts of misanthropy.

For much of the time, at least in his writing, Van

[4] For braver attempts at creating theories of desert aesthetics, see Dutton (140–56), Perkins (42–47, 96–97, 158), and Banham (208–28). Helpful for their larger contexts are the more general works of Bachelard and Tuan.

Dyke kept his inner turmoil under control. At other moments, pure bile flowed from his pen. In the fortunately forgotten *The Money God: Chapters of Heresy and Dissent Concerning Business Methods and Mercenary Ideals in American Life*, wealthy Van Dyke rends his garments and gnashes his teeth at the stupidities of his fellow men. Laborers are overpaid and demanding more, businessmen greedy, professors corrupt, dull-eyed immigrants reek with cabbage smells. . . . On and on Van Dyke rages, catching just about everyone, every class, profession, every division and category of society, in his sights—except his friend and benefactor Andrew Carnegie, who, in Van Dyke's view, is the very paragon of human light. For those who remember *The Desert* as a book of fine-tuned poetic soarings, *The Money God* is a shocking work, a bewildering tirade. Elsewhere, Van Dyke expresses his ire more carefully, snidely mocking dull-witted tourists who sit on the terrace of their Cairo hotel and, with nothing better to do, gawk at the passing traffic as they "suck the paint off the handles of their canes" (*In Egypt* 15). However he channels it, the anger is always there. Much of Van Dyke's writing is driven by the sulfurous churnings in his soul.

All of this would be neither here nor there, the writer's motives for writing being more the province of the psychologist, not of the literary historian, except that this darker side of Van Dyke has everything to do with the shape of the book you now hold. And not only the shape but with the reasons for taking the very trip which produced the book.

One could think, for instance, that as adherents of Art for Art's Sake glowed with beauty, part of their joie would be a generous concern for mankind. For some, this was undoubtedly true. For others, however, art was the opposite, an escape from a doomed world. Picture the wealthy connoisseur sitting in his study at night. For all his fine talk and public good deeds, he has blood on his hands, for he is ruthless in his dealings, both with his workers and with his fellow industrialists. The beauty of the pictures around him can blot out, if for the moment, the unsolvable ills and nastiness of his daily life. But total escape is not possible; beyond lies the waiting world.

We tend to forget that much of what we think of as culture—our symphony orchestras, great art museums, and such—had their provenance in the closing decades of the nineteenth century. In concept, these were luxuries transported from Europe, and they were made possible in large part by the wealthy leaders of industrializing America, members of the only class that then could afford them. Such was their release from the sordid world around them, a world largely of their creation. And it was not a pleasant one. Around Carnegie's factories, ghettoes teemed with illiterate Italians, Greeks, and Slavs—the cheap immigrant labor straining twelve and sometimes sixteen hours a day at the wheels of the great, new steel factories. Those factories, of course, not only shaved off arms and created many a widow, they belched constant plumes of smoke coating cities in soot. Urban America was turning into a fetid trash dump. The well-off might escape on vacations to country homes, but on their return there it was, worse than before—unwashed, crime-ridden masses living in filth, the dregs of humanity, and, so it was believed by many who shook their heads, as unchangeable in their slovenly habits as pigs in a sty. In passing through, one could only lift his skirts and hope their hems escaped permanent stain. Adding more generally to the malaise was the cynicism spawned by Darwin and the doubt gnawing ever more aggressively in the collective soul that, if not dead, God was slumbering at the levers of the universe.

Although some light-filled leaders, at least, took action as concerns the earthly realm, urging progressive solutions in education and innovative labor policies, nineteenth-century optimism had its dark side. Many men in power simply accepted theological doubts as inoperable and, regarding daily affairs down here, turned their backs on the noxious social problems. The artists and intellectuals they supported sometimes shared their disdain. Among them was John C. Van Dyke. About God he had little to say, except, by implication, that the universe was a hostile if beautiful machine eventually grinding up poetic souls in its lovely maws. As to more mundane issues of daily intercourse, Van Dyke stroked his highly developed sensibilities and rarely hesitated to express his horror at the hoi polloi and its rank kitchen smells. The Afterlife likely was a black void, but in this one to save himself the aesthete must eschew anything that smacked "of popular interest" (*What Is Art* 87) and flee the popular realism that is "the lowest and most contemptible form of art" (*Principles of Art* 176).

That's why, when he sent the manuscript of *The Desert* to his editor at Scribner's, Van Dyke included a note. The book, he sniffed to William C. Brownell, is "a whole lot better than the swash which today is being turned out as 'literature.' And it will sell, too; but not up in the hundreds of thousands. It is not so bad as that. My audience is only a few thousand, thank God."[5] Thus, the writer of *The Desert* looked

---

[5] John C. Van Dyke to William C. Brownell, 23 May 1901 (Teague and Wild 39–40).

down his snoot at the world. On this, there can be no doubt. A few years before he traveled to the Southwest, with typical acid Van Dyke wrote fellow art critic Kenyon Cox, assuring him that because of stupidity the mass of people cannot grasp the fine points of books. The public, Van Dyke snorted, "is a great ass of some booby."[6]

Then why would he even bother, as he did in *The Desert*, to make a pretense of inviting the weary urban masses to follow him out into the succor of the wilderness? Ah, that was part of an elaborate snub—and, more than that, proof in Van Dyke's mind of the very gullibility of the masses he despised. And it was not at all a one-time ruse, the kind of blunder that many a writer might make and then regret. In book after book this chronically ill professor, who often was so frail he couldn't mount the lecture platform, ascribes to himself colorful acts of derring-do as he rides manfully after buffalo with a tribe of "wild" Indians, gets the drop on outlaws, and outshoots fellow cowpokes—all while laughing up his sleeve at the believing public. To such an extent that elder brother Theodore grew hot under the collar at the lies and tried to dissuade Van Dyke from his

---

[6] John C. Van Dyke to Kenyon Cox, 29 April 1893 (Teague and Wild 108–9).

tomfoolery, but by then Van Dyke was dizzy with his tricks and out of control.[7]

In the case of *The Desert*, Van Dyke executes the perversity in his most complex subterfuge. He begins by dedicating the book not to John Muir or some other earnest nature-lover of the day but to Andrew Carnegie, one of the nation's great nature-wreckers, here masked by the initials A. M. C. On top of that, a close reading of the preface shows that its "you"— those invited by the author to travel with him through desert exhilarations—is not the general reading audience, which for decades glowed with the flattery of the writer's direct address, but Carnegie and his coterie of art aficionados. Only they, according to the underlying message, have the sensibilities to appreciate the delicacy of the prose that follows (Ingham and Wild).

What follows, however one might choose to carp at Van Dyke, is a masterpiece of lyricism. With a force sometimes approaching madness, Van Dyke overwhelms his subject, "painting" his vision of the desert in terms of the wild colors and druidical waywardness of J. M. W. Turner, an English artist much admired by Van Dyke who, indeed, went

[7] The correspondence is in the possession of a Van Dyke relative. Copies are in the archives of the Mojave Desert Heritage and Cultural Association, Goffs, California.

slowly mad.[8] Yet, as is immediately evident from the meticulous detail of Van Dyke's table of contents, the writer serves all this up in a tight, quite rational structure, with the book moving smartly along from a section on mirages to chapters on cactus and wild-life, even while his wildness insistently breaks the formal restraints. Thus, in rhetorical terms, the appealing tug of lyricism and order, romanticism and classicism, emotion and reason.

This moving performance, however, comes with a large caveat. Although, pointing with his fescue, Van Dyke assumes a classroom tone in describing the desert's plants and animals, he was no naturalist. The depictions of the outdoors by this familiar of salons can be wildly inaccurate, declaring coyotes lazy, getting the blossom of the giant cactus the wrong color, and—reader beware—dubbing the rattlesnake all but harmless. Many of the facts Van Dyke did get straight about the desert he probably gleaned from his much-admired brother Theodore, who was a legitimate outdoors writer and later a rancher in the Mojave Desert of Southern California and knew what he was talking about, as the visiting professor did not.

---

[8] Teague and Wild 7–10; Wild "How a London Madman Painted Our Deserts."

Yet, in a sense, Van Dyke's *sans souci* attitude as he flings his "facts" around is entirely consistent with his aesthetic and, as well, part and parcel of his intended snub. After all, he had every right to exaggerate, using words to paint his impression of the desert in any way he wished; the problem occurs because he misleads readers into believing that he is presenting, not an artistic vision, but a realistic account of the desert. In sum, the lover of beauty had little patience with the bean counters, with those so déclassé as to care about the details of mere fact, of mere science. His mind was on a higher plane, disported itself in more ethereal realms (Wild and Carmony).[9]

It should be added for the sake of a larger context that such slipperiness with the truth was not unusual for travel books of the time, especially books about the "Wild West." That roisterous region, fascinating to Easterners, invited writers to spin tall tales in exchange for the prospect of increased sales. How-

[9] Aesthetically, Van Dyke lived in an insubstantial, if alluring, world of wraiths. *The Desert* was one of six books in a series exploring the visual delights of nature's "appearances," the loveliness of her aspects in mountains, oceans, and so on. Aficionados of the desert, however, may be disappointed. In these and other books, Van Dyke's tendency is to praise whatever scenery lies before him as the most beautiful he has ever seen (Wild "A Western Sun Sets in the East").

ever, that does not excuse Van Dyke. All the more egregious is the yielding to this temptation by a man who publicly touted his own sterling rectitude. Compounding the issue, there was no good reason for the sloppiness and falsification other than Van Dyke's thumbing his nose at the public, for with his talents and colorful subject he could have written a book both accurate and poetically compelling. In brief, *The Desert* didn't need such shenanigans.

Since larger issues are under consideration, the caveat extends to some of Van Dyke's famous passages. Today's desert lovers, thinking Van Dyke in the front ranks of conservationists, often quote what seems to be the author's stentorian pitch for preserving the arid lands: "The deserts should never be reclaimed. They are the breathing-spaces of the west and should be preserved forever" (59). At the time, great debate was raging over whether or not irrigation projects, planned on grand scales for the arid lands, would change the desert's climate, charging it with humidity, and thus ruining its curative powers for health-seekers such as Van Dyke. By "breathing-spaces," then, Van Dyke is not talking metaphorically, about preserving the desert so that people might have room to wander and enjoy nature, but is speaking quite literally, about protecting the quality of the air for the relief of his own respiratory problems. True, the passage occurs amid several pages of heated and superbly effective rhetoric in which the author storms over abuses to America's landscapes. Van Dyke had the ability to work himself up into a fine, crowd-pleasing candescence when such a performance served his purposes. These pages may ring with much of the imagery and tone of John Muir's earlier "The American Forests," but unlike great conservationist Muir, Van Dyke lifted nary a finger to back up his fine sentiments with action.[10]

In any case, with *The Desert* Van Dyke was doing what he often did when he traveled, writing a book about the beauty around him—or, better put, about his perception of the beauty around him. And that's exactly the thrill readers get and the charged fascination blinding them through the decades to the book's many factual slips—a view of nature by an upper-class aesthete flying on his romantic wings. From his privileged position, Van Dyke swoons over

[10] Despite this, Van Dyke made much of his acquaintance with Muir, claiming in his autobiography that Muir had traveled to the Mojave ranch just to meet him (167). Quite likely, Muir was there to visit his daughter Helen, who was living at the desert ranch because of her health. Also likely closer to the truth, according to Van Dyke's nephew Dix Van Dyke, a hand at the ranch, when Muir and Van Dyke met, they quarreled (135).

an imagined art-deco world of lavender lizards flitting through one's consciousness, a world supercharged with beauty, where the very air is colored. With such language, Van Dyke gave us the vocabulary, however misrepresentative, that we use today, the *Arizona Highways* vocabulary turning a harsh place into a lush, exciting landscape.

As mentioned earlier, Van Dyke came at just the right time. His was the first book devoted to praising the desert, and that this work immediately took fire with the public needs a brief background. No sooner had Americans conquered the wilderness, cut down the forests, and slaughtered the buffalo than the romantic nation began sentimentalizing the past, longing for what it had just destroyed. Now as cities grew and the surrounding countryside was reduced to fields of stumps, people yearned for what they perceived as the freer and more harmonious life of their ancestors, lived closer to nature. That is, the bored, industrialized nation of offices and smokestacks and streets lined with brick row homes was longing for the exotic (Nash). A vigorous corollary resulted from the widespread fear that, cut off from our pioneer heritage, the nation was going soft. Thus, the birth of the Boy Scouts and other national organizations plunging youth back into the outdoors.

A famed outdoorsman took up the torch. In speech after speech, President Theodore Roosevelt exhorted the nation to regain its muscles by living what he labeled The Strenuous Life.

Coming precisely at the right time, hyperactive, hyperenthusiastic Van Dyke told worried Americans about a romantic and exotic place where they might renew themselves. With a grand, dramatic gesture, he pointed to a land where the wolves still howled as a globose moon tore through the silver clouds, to an uninhabited region of endless enchantments awaiting them, out there in the long-ignored deserts of the Southwest. Dotted with ranches and crisscrossed by fences, the region hardly was as wild as the professor made it out to be, but what he said was just what people wanted to hear, and in several ways of looking at it, Van Dyke was right.

Slowly, even before Van Dyke, the bane of pioneers, that region of waterholes ringed by travelers' bones and haunt of marauding Indians, had been getting a second look. Technology and an iron-fisted government had made this possible. By Van Dyke's time, the U.S. Cavalry had made the deserts safe from the Indian attacks widely repeated in pioneer lore, and the railroads had followed, reducing travel across the sand dunes to a pleasant excursion of a few hours rather than a grueling, weeks-long trek behind teetering oxen. Among the early enthusiasts were the sick. In the days before antibiotics, respiratory problems plagued the nation, condemning thousands of people to slow, choking, coughing deaths. None other than Van Dyke's brother Theodore had moved to southern California in a desperate search for health. He, along with thousands of other hacking and blood-spitting invalids, discovered that in the clean, dry air, in that year-long summer—why, he could breathe again! And people whose very lives are saved, blessed by the climate of a place, soon become lifetime boosters.

The desert offered other riches besides health. There oranges and pomegranates, limes and other fruits known only from Sinbad tales, held out their acrylic globes for the picking. And there was gold, millions and millions of dollars of gold and silver, pouring out of the hills. And Indians (thankfully pacified) dancing on mesa tops to bring the rain. Why, this was a fabulous place, of health and wealth and exotic spiritual auras.[11] This was precisely what such desert converts as Charles F. Lummis and Mary Austin were saying years before John C. Van Dyke ever saw a sand dune. Van Dyke's luck, however, was

[11] We are fortunate for W. Storrs Lee's *The Great California Deserts*, which follows the shifting image of the desert as a wasteland to that of a dreamland.

that up until then no one had sung an epithalamium
to the desert between the covers of one book. Not
only did Van Dyke say it best; armed with his
invaluable connections to Scribner's, he said it first.
For these two circumstances—and the colorful leg-
ends surrounding his personality—Van Dyke and
his book became foremost desert icons.

There remains, however, one large issue surrounding both the man and his famous book, a slippery
and intriguing one, indeed—and all the more intriguing because it likely will never be fully explained.
What was this habitué of glittering social circles
doing wandering around in the desert to begin with?

We know this much from letters and other solid
documentation. For much of his life Van Dyke was
wracked by a variety of chronic maladies, among
them respiratory problems. It would be only natural
for him to seek relief, as had his brother, from the
cold and damp of winters back East in the healing
air of the Southwest. We know, too, that periodically
over the decades he visited brother Theodore, first in
Los Angeles and then at Theodore's ranch near
Daggett, far out in the Mojave Desert. To judge from
this, Van Dyke's trip through the arid regions hardly
was one long foray, as presented in his book, but a
series of quite civilized excursions in Derby hat and
necktie, opportunities for his writer's mind to process

what he saw into the "enchanted" landscapes of *The Desert* (xx). That is, Van Dyke was a writer traveling for the dual purposes of visiting his brother and improving his health.

After that, the story becomes fishy, especially when we combine what we know about Van Dyke with the always suspect information this weaver of fantasies passes on about himself. His *Autobiography*, for instance, states that he was seeking health in the Southwest, then adds a typical Van Dykean flare to events: "I was just ill enough not to care much about perils and morbid enough to prefer dying in the sand alone to passing out in a hotel with a room maid weeping at the foot of the bed" (118). Next he tells us he straps on his pistol and, with a peal of madcap laughter, rides off into the great unknown. For certain, dramatic reading, but for that the scene smacks more of Van Dyke's usual literary smoke than of actual events.

Probing beyond exaggeration into Van Dyke's life casts an entirely new light on his Southwestern trips. Even his *Autobiography* hints at this. Wandering alone in Mexico, he says he wants to return to New Jersey, but he can't because "there seemed no alternative" (122). That rings false. The truth is that at almost any point in his travels he could have hopped on a train and been back home in a matter of days. Bearing on this, Van Dyke's letters from New Brunswick to his editor at Scribner's narrow the meaning. Several times Van Dyke complains about the heat in his college town, for instance: "The heat is infernal and I want to get out fast."[12] Clearly, Van Dyke is speaking metaphorically to his editor, for where is Van Dyke going but to Wilkes-Barre, Pennsylvania, only about a hundred miles inland from New Brunswick and hardly a refuge from a heat wave. With little doubt, at times Van Dyke left New Brunswick, not for pleasure or health, but to escape the "heat" of a personal problem rubbing him raw.

The situation is further clarified with the testimony of a Van Dyke relative. As it happened, bachelor Van Dyke had a daughter, Clare, with the wife of a fellow faculty member at Rutgers (Strong x–xi). Family anecdote has it that Clare periodically became feisty in her teenage years and, at least once, insisted on packing her bags and moving in with her biological father, who lived across the street from Rutgers up on the "Holy Hill" of the seminary campus. Whether or not Clare actually carried out her threat is unknown, but, in any case, this was not a comforting situation brewing at one of America's premiere

[12] John C. Van Dyke to William C. Brownell, 2 June 1902 or 1903 (Teague and Wild 42).

religious institutions, where Van Dyke was the head librarian. Still, much of this is in the nature of hearsay, and, despite the patterns of intrigue lying behind the surface of Van Dyke's career, one needs to be careful about being cozened by colorful possibilities.

That we're not being cozened comes clear, somewhat astoundingly, from a document bearing the handwriting not only of Van Dyke but also of that archmaster of double-dealings, his friend and mentor Andrew Carnegie. It should be said in this regard that among the many angles of the professor's personality was a fortunate eccentricity. Although he often played his cards close to the vest when it came to the details of both his real and his imagined affairs, at times he did a puzzling thing. He left a seemingly deliberate clue here and there, as if he wished to be followed on his crinkum-crankum trail, albeit taking some pleasure in advance by putting future scholars through their paces.

The best example bearing on Van Dyke's desert travels is a letter written to him by Andrew Carnegie and preserved in Van Dyke's personal scrapbook, in the archives of the seminary. At first glance, Carnegie's typewritten note seems unremarkable, a chatty little letter saying how sorry Lady Waterlow will be that Van Dyke will not be stopping by

Carnegie's castle in Scotland this summer and hop-
ing that Van Dyke will be able to make it over for
some fishing in October. It is just the sort of phatic
utterance one sees time after time in the correspondence of men who, whatever their underhanded
nastiness in piling up fortunes, minded their p's and
q's in matters of etiquette. To one side at the top,
however, Van Dyke has written a strange notation:
"This is the letter in which A. C. wrote in pencil to
give McLuckie all the money he wanted and to 'rub
this out.'" An arrow points to a smudge in the left-
hand margin. The message indeed is erased, but
with a magnifying glass one can make out the last
words, "rub this out."[13]

McLuckie, it turns out, was John McLuckie, a
leader in the Homestead Strike of 1892. This, among
the bloodiest conflicts in American labor history,
took place at one of Carnegie's steel mills near
Pittsburgh. Though the workers were crushed into
submission, in the following years reformer McLuckie
caused Carnegie considerable grief by mounting the
stump and not letting the public forget the steel
magnate's vicious handling of the affair. So much so
that the former striker, hounded by Carnegie's agents,

[13] Andrew Carnegie to John C. Van Dyke, 29 June 1898
(Teague and Wild 127–28).

fled for his life to Mexico. Without recounting all the twists and turns in the labyrinths of this tawdry affair, it appears quite clear that Carnegie was using Van Dyke as a bagman, sending him deep into Mexico to pay off McLuckie and silence him with a substantial bribe (Wild "The Homestead Strike and the Mexican Connection").

Van Dyke, we should remember, was a privileged man who throve on plots and intricate schemes. As holds true for so many aspects of his complex life, Van Dyke visited the Southwest periodically for a number of reasons, to breathe its clear air, visit his brother, escape the scandal caused by Clare, and, while he was at it, do a little favor for the richest man in America. And yes, while there he wrote another volume about nature's beauty. One notes, for example, that Van Dyke dates his Preface-Dedication to *The Desert* from La Noria Verde, the magnificent hacienda in Mexico where the tryst with McLuckie took place (xxi).

Such are the origins of the most famous volume on America's deserts.[14] In this, we have a curious

[14] Added to this swirl is, of all things, the strong possibility of a French connection, through the wildly popular and eminently debauched novelist Pierre Loti. See my "Viewing America's Deserts, Part 1," as well as Loti's undated note to Van Dyke (Teague and Wild 130–31).

match. Our modern, intensely urbanized, although
for all that highly romantic, mass society yearns for a
romanticized desert, a place of mystery where the
soul can play. The heart finds its answer in a book of
beautiful illusions struck off by a well-off aesthete
panting after the excitements of smoke and mirrors.
Beneath the layer of its colorful airiness, however,
this is a profound book, in both its vision and
cultural effect. Not only was this American Land
Classic immediately popular, but, as we've observed, the incredible longevity of *The Desert* has
steeped generations down to this day in the book's
vocabulary of desert appreciation. Deeper still, whatever its flaws, Van Dyke's volume deals with those
issues of fantasy and reality, truth and beauty,
which, as Keats reminds us, are aspects of life few of
us wish to abandon.

The text reproduced in this reprint is the original
edition of *The Desert*, first published in September
1901.[15] The dramatic frontispiece, titled *Silence and*

---

[15] The publishing history of *The Desert*, with its many reprints,
several editions, and various formats, should delight bibliogra-
phers avid for challenges. A thorough job—a formidable task—of
comparing the numerous texts, including the two recent offerings
mentioned below, still waits to be done (Teague and Wild 41, n. 4;
42–43, n. 8). Nevertheless, several telling nuggets emerge from
the tangle.

Desolation, also reproduced from Van Dyke's original, joins other slippery issues surrounding the
book. In his *Wonders of the Colorado Desert*, George

Soon after the appearance of *The Desert*, Robert H. Forbes, a
professor of agriculture at the University of Arizona, apparently
challenged Van Dyke over his numerous faux pas in natural
history. We do not have Professor Forbes' original letter, but Van
Dyke's response, one of the longest letters he ever wrote, is a
marvel, a squidlike performance of wheedling and ducking (John
C. Van Dyke to Robert H. Forbes, 4 November 1901. Teague and
Wild 6–7, 59–61). Reacting to Forbes' admonishments, Van Dyke
made a few, mostly minor, changes in the 1903 reprint, but he
didn't bother to correct many of his errors in this and following
reprints and editions—a reaction totally consistent with Van
Dyke's cavalier ways.

Two further changes are worthy of special note. In 1918,
Scribner's issued an edition featuring photographs of the desert by
California writer J. Smeaton Chase; possibly mixed among them
are some of Van Dyke's own photographic work. The illustrations
appeared in several reprints thereafter and likely fostered sales.
However successful commercially, the ploy violated Van Dyke's
aesthetic abhorrence of realism, a violation he enthusiastically
endorsed in his letters supporting this edition (Teague and Wild
11–12, 43–44, 45–53).

In 1930, two years before Van Dyke's death, nephew Dix Van
Dyke agreed to a request by Scribner's and appended a set of
natural-history notes to the famous book. However, likely in
deference to his aging uncle, Dix, although a man well acquainted
with desert things, tiptoed around most of the book's obvious
flaws.

Professors Powell and Shelton each wrote introductions for
modern reprints of *The Desert*.

Wharton James boldly accused rival desert writer Van Dyke of stealing the picture from him (1: xxix).

I hope that the Index, the first ever created for the text of *The Desert*, will prove a special help.

Readers taken by this brief portrait of Van Dyke and *The Desert* are fortunate, for a rich trove of Van Dyke's works awaits them. Not only did he write dozens upon dozens of books. We watch as his volumes about the beauty of the outdoors race up and down the scales, ranging from flights into the sublime to the bitterest depressions, from manly adventures in the frontier West to vignettes of Van Dyke's friends Mark Twain, Theodore Roosevelt, and James McNeill Whistler. Chief among such pleasures is the bared-claws catfight between Van Dyke and novelist Edith Wharton. The fur flew for years, each earnest antagonist giving good measure for measure because, well, because in a way these two high-strung writers were made for each other. Readers might plunge in just about anywhere in these books and read happily on. Here, however, are a few suggestions.

A companion book to *The Desert* is *The Open Spaces*. Although, as Van Dyke admitted to his brother, this is his "big lie" about hard riding and quick shooting on the frontier, it is eminently readable. Similarly, the first chapter in *The Mountain* recounts a summer-long boyhood buffalo hunt with a band of Sioux Indians. Here, a young Van Dyke riding bareback dashes off with his friends, flying over coulees and dangerous outcrops, over the Great Plains clear to the Rocky Mountains in breathless pursuit of winter meat. Almost surely pure fantasy, but it is, nevertheless, the most gripping account of a buffalo hunt I've ever read.

Van Dyke's *Autobiography* offers more sophisticated reading. Again, in his wayward manner Van Dyke can swing far from veracity, and, creating, I hope, an instructive tension, my notes for the book keep pulling him back to the facts of his life. For all that, Van Dyke draws striking portraits which ring true for the artists, writers, and wealthy playboys (and their ladies) of the late Victorian age. The autobiography also contains a substantial bibliography of primary and secondary sources. Related to this, friend and colleague David Teague and I recently edited *The Secret Life of John C. Van Dyke*, a collection of Van Dyke's letters. Here, if anywhere, the truth we seek about a writer leaps to the fore—a truth that sometimes can be shocking.

To his credit, Van Dyke could shift gears, creating a sustained work in appealing sepia. In the midst of all the Sturm und Drang on which the tortured Van

Dyke thrives—and maybe because of it—my own preference is for *The Meadows*, a quiet and deliciously nostalgic tribute to the woodlands and meadows surrounding the idyllic college town of New Brunswick. Here the harried writer, plagued by turmoil and personal troubles (many of them of his own making), wanders, his own Thoreau, through fields and forest, aesthetically inspecting the new snow weighing down spruce trees, chuckling at the antics of squirrels, and wondering at the geese overhead. Then turning, looking back at the college spires rising through the town's great trees, he could believe, if only for the moment, that nature's beauty, indeed, is a torn life's greatest balm.

Lastly, for an outside view of Van Dyke we are fortunate to have a book of reminiscences by Theodore's son, rough-and-ready rancher Dix Van Dyke. In *Daggett: Life in a Mojave Frontier Town* we see not only a wild boom town of gunslingers and drunken miners dragged kicking and screaming into the twentieth century. We enjoy the curious contrast of craggy rancher Theodore and his rough-and-tumble world with the refined professor who often visited the ranch, where, as earlier mentioned, moaning ghosts still wander.

WORKS CITED

Bachelard, Gaston. *The Poetics of Space*. Trans. Maria Jolas. 1958. Reprint, Boston: Beacon Press, 1969.

Banham, Peter Reyner. *Scenes in America Deserta*. Salt Lake City: Gibbs M. Smith, 1982.

Dutton, Clarence E. *The Tertiary History of the Grand Cañon District*. 1882. Reprint, Santa Barbara: Peregrine Smith, 1977.

Ingham, Zita, and Peter Wild. "The Preface as Illumination: The Curious (If Not Tricky) Case of John C. Van Dyke's *The Desert*." *Rhetoric Review* 9 (1991): 328–39.

James, George Wharton. *The Wonders of the Colorado Desert*. 2 vols. Boston: Little, Brown, 1906.

Lee, W. Storrs. *The Great California Deserts*. New York: Putnam's, 1963.

Muir, John. "The American Forests." *Atlantic Monthly* 80, no. 478 (August 1897): 145–57.

Nash, Roderick. *Wilderness and the American Mind*. 3d ed. New Haven: Yale University Press, 1982.

Perkins, Edna Brush. *The White Heart of Mojave*. New York: Boni and Liveright, 1922.

Powell, Lawrence Clark. *Southwest Classics: The Creative Literature of the Arid Lands*. 1974. Reprint, Tucson: University of Arizona Press, 1982.

Roosevelt, Theodore. "The Strenuous Life." *The Strenuous Life: Essays and Addresses*. New York: Century, 1902. 1–21.

Shelton, Richard. Introduction to *The Desert*, by John C. Van Dyke. Salt Lake City: Peregrine Smith, 1980. xi–xxix.

Strong, Philip L. Foreword to *The Autobiography of John C. Van Dyke: A Personal Narrative of American Life, 1861–1931*. Ed. Peter Wild. Salt Lake City: University of Utah Press, 1993. vii–xi.

Teague, David, and Peter Wild, eds. *The Secret Life of John C. Van Dyke: Selected Letters*. Reno: University of Nevada Press, 1997.

Tuan, Yi-Fu. *Topophilia: A Study of Environmental Perception, Attitudes, and Values*. Englewood Cliffs: Prentice-Hall, 1974.

Van Dyke, Dix. *Daggett: Life in a Mojave Frontier Town*. Ed. Peter Wild. Baltimore: Johns Hopkins University Press, 1997.

Van Dyke, John C. *The Autobiography of John C. Van Dyke: A Personal Narrative of American Life, 1861–1931*. Ed. Peter Wild. Salt Lake City: University of Utah Press, 1993.

———. *The Desert: Further Studies in Natural Appearances*. New York: Scribner's, 1901.

———. *The Desert: Further Studies in Natural Appearances*. Introduction by Lawrence Clark Powell. Tucson: The Arizona Historical Society, 1976.

———. *The Desert: Further Studies in Natural Appearances*. Introduction by Richard Shelton. Salt Lake City: Peregrine Smith, 1980.

———. *The Desert: Further Studies in Natural Appearances*. Notes by Dix Van Dyke. New York: Scribner's, 1930.

———. *The Desert: Further Studies in Natural Appearances*. Photographs by J. Smeaton Chase. New York: Scribner's, 1918.

————. *In Egypt: Studies and Sketches along the Nile*. New York: Scribner's, 1931.

————. *The Meadows: Familiar Studies of the Commonplace*. New York: Scribner's, 1926.

————. *The Money God: Chapters of Heresy and Dissent Concerning Business Methods and Mercenary Ideals in American Life*. New York: Scribner's, 1908.

————. *The Mountain: Renewed Studies in Impressions and Appearances*. New York: Scribner's, 1916.

————. *The Open Spaces: Incidents of Nights and Days Under the Blue Sky*. New York: Scribner's, 1922.

————. *Principles of Art*. New York: Fords, Howard, and Hulbert, 1887.

————. *What Is Art?: Studies in the Technique and Criticism of Painting*. New York: Scribner's, 1910.

Wild, Peter. "The Homestead Strike and the Mexican Connection: The Strange Story of 'Honest' John McLuckie." *Pittsburgh History* 80, no. 2 (summer 1997): 60–9, 74.

————. "How a London Madman Painted Our Deserts." *North Dakota Quarterly* 63, no. 2 (spring 1996): 5–17.

————. "Viewing America's Deserts, Part 1: John C. Van Dyke and the French Connection." *Puerto del Sol* 26, no. 2 (1991): 58–78.

————. "A Western Sun Sets in the East: The Five 'Appearances' Surrounding John C. Van Dyke's *The Desert*." *Western American Literature* 25 (1990): 218–31.

Wild, Peter, and Neil Carmony. "The Trip Not Taken." *Journal of Arizona History* 34, no. 1 (spring 1993): 65–80.

THE DESERT

Silence and Desolation

THE DESERT

CHAPTER I

THE APPROACH

IT is the last considerable group of mountains
between the divide and the low basin of the
Colorado desert. For days I have been watching them change color at sunset—watching the
canyons shift into great slashes of blue and
purple shadow, and the ridges flame with edgings of glittering fire. They are lonesome looking mountains lying off there by themselves on
the plain, so still, so barren, so blazing hot
under the sun. Forsaken of their kind, one
might not inappropriately call them the "Lost
Mountains"—the surviving remnant no doubt
of some noble range that long centuries ago
was beaten by wind and rain into desert sand.
And yet before one gets to them they may prove
quite formidable heights, with precipitous sides
and unsurmountable tops. Who knows? Not
those with whom I am stopping, for they have

*Desert
mountains.*

1

not been there. They do not even know the name of them. The Papagoes leave them alone because there is no game in them. Evidently they are considered unimportant hills, nobody's hills, no man's range; but nevertheless I am off for them in the morning at daylight.

Unknown ranges.

I ride away through the thin mesquite and the little adobe ranch house is soon lost to view. The morning is still and perfectly clear. The stars have gone out, the moon is looking pale, the deep blue is warming, the sky is lightening with the coming day. How cool and crystalline the air ! In a few hours the great plain will be almost like a fiery furnace under the rays of the summer sun, but now it is chilly. And in a few hours there will be rings and bands and scarves of heat set wavering across the waste upon the opalescent wings of the mirage; but now the air is so clear that one can see the breaks in the rocky face of the mountain range, though it is fully twenty miles away. It may be further. Who of the desert has not spent his day riding at a mountain and never even reaching its base ? This is a land of illusions and thin air. The vision is so cleared at times that the truth itself is deceptive. But I shall ride on for several hours. If, by twelve

Early morning on the desert.

Air illusions.

o'clock, the foot hills are not reached, I shall turn back.

The summer heat has withered everything except the mesquite, the palo verde,* the grease wood, and the various cacti. Under foot there is a little dry grass, but more often patches of bare gravel and sand rolled in shallow beds that course toward the large valleys. *Sand forms in the valleys.* In the draws and flat places the fine sand lies thicker, is tossed in wave forms by the wind, and banked high against clumps of cholla or prickly pear. In the wash-outs and over the cut banks of the arroyos it is sometimes heaped in mounds and crests like driven snow. It blows here along the boundary line between Arizona and Sonora almost every day ; and the tailing of the sands behind the bushes shows that the prevailing winds are from the Gulf *Winds of the desert.* region. A cool wind ? Yes, but only by comparison with the north wind. When you feel it on your face you may think it the breath of some distant volcano.

How pale - blue the Lost Mountains look under the growing light. I am watching their edges develop into broken barriers of rock, and

* The use of Spanish names is compulsory. There are no English equivalents.

Sun shafts.

even as I watch the tallest tower of all is struck with a bright fawn color. It is the high point to catch the first shaft of the sun. Quickly the light spreads downward until the whole ridge is tinged by it, and the abrupt sides of porphyry begin to glow under it. It is not long before great shafts of light alternating with shadow stretch down the plain ahead of me. The sun is streaming through the tops of the eastern mountains and the sharp pointed pinnacles are cutting shadows in the broad beam of light.

That beam of light! Was there ever anything so beautiful! How it flashes its color through shadow, how it gilds the tops of the mountains and gleams white on the dunes of the desert! In any land what is there more glorious than sunlight! Even here in the desert, where it falls fierce and hot as a rain of meteors, it is the one supreme beauty to which all things pay allegiance. The beast and the bird are not too fond of its heat and as soon as the sun is high in the heavens they seek cover in the canyons; but for all that the chief glory of the desert is its broad blaze of omnipresent light.

The beauty of sunlight.

Yes, there is animal and bird life here though it is not always apparent unless you look for it.

Wrens and linnets are building nests in the cholla, and finches are singing from the top of the sahuaro.* There are plenty of reptiles, *Desert life.* rabbits and ground squirrels quietly slipping out of your way; and now that the sun is up you can see a long sun-burned slant-of-hair trotting up yonder divide and casting an apprehensive head from side to side as he moves off. It is not often that the old gray wolf shows himself to the traveller. He is usually up in the mountains before sunrise. And seldom now does one see the desert antelope along the *Antelope.* mesas, and yet off to the south you can see patches of white that come and go almost like flashing mirrors in the sun. They are stragglers from some band that have drifted up from central Sonora. No; they are not far away. A little mirage is already forming over that portion of the mesa and makes them look more distant than they are in reality. You can be deceived on the desert by the nearness of things quite as often as by their remoteness.

These desert mountains have a fashion of appearing distant until you are almost up to them. Then they seem to give up the game of decep- *The Lost Mountains.* tion and come out of their hiding-places. It is

* Properly Saguaro.

just so with the mountains toward which I am riding. After several hours they seem to rise up suddenly in front of me and I am at their base. They are not high—perhaps fifteen hundred feet. The side near me is precipitous rock, weather-stained to a reddish-black. A ride around the bases discloses an almost complete perpendicular wall, slanting off half way down the sides into sloping beds of bowlders that have been shaken loose from the upper strata. A huge cleft in the western side—half barranca half canyon—seems to suggest a way to the summit.

Mountain walls.

The walking up the mountain is not the best in the world. It is over splintered rock, stepping from stone to stone, creeping along the backbone of bowlders, and worrying over rows of granite blocks. Presently the course seems to slip into a diagonal—a winding up and around the mountain—and ahead of me the stones begin to look peculiar, almost familiar. There seems to be a trail over the ledges and through the broken blocks ; but what should make a trail up that deserted mountain ? Mule-deer travelling toward the summit to lie down in the heat of the day ? It is possible. The track of a band of deer soon becomes a

The ascent.

Deer trails.

beaten path, and animals are just as fond of a good path as humanity. By a strange coincidence at this very moment the sharp-toed print of a deer's hoof appears in the ground before me. But it looks a little odd. The impression is so clear cut that I stoop to examine it. It is with no little astonishment that I find it sunk in stone instead of earth—petrified in rock and overrun with silica. The bare suggestion gives one pause. How many thousands *Footprints.* of years ago was that impression stamped upon the stone ? By what strange chance has it survived destruction ? And while it remains quite perfect to-day—the vagrant hoof-mark of a desert deer—what has become of the once carefully guarded footprints of the Sargons, the Pharaohs and the Cæsars ? With what contempt Nature sometimes plans the survival of the least fit, and breaks the conqueror on his shield !

Further up the mountain the deer-trail theory is abandoned—at least so far as recent times are concerned. The stones are worn too smooth, *The stone path.* the larger ones have been pushed aside by something more intelligent than a mule-deer's hoof ; and in one place the trail seems to have been built up on the descending side. There is not the slightest evidence, either by rub upon the rocks, or overturned stones, or scrape in the gravel, that any living thing has passed up this pathway for many years ; and yet the trail is a distinct line of lighter colored stone stretch-

Following the trail. ing ahead of me. It is a path worn in the rocks, and there is no grass or vine or weed to obliterate it. It leads on and up to the saddle of the mountain. There is a crevasse or chasm breaking through this saddle which might have been bridged at one time with mesquite trunks, but is now to be leaped if one would reach the summit. It is narrow only in one place and this is just where the trail happens to run. Across it, on the upper side, there is a horse-

Defensive walls. shoe shaped enclosure of stone. It is only a few feet in diameter, and the upper layers of stone have fallen ; but the little wall still stands as high as one's waist. Could this have been a sentinel box used to guard the passage of the trail at this place ?

Higher and still higher until at last the mountain broadens into a flat top. I am so eager to gain the height and am expecting so much that at first I overlook what is before me.

The summit. Gradually I make out a long parapet of loose stone on the trail side of the mountain which joins on to steep cliffs on the other sides.   A conclusion is instantly jumped at, for the imagination will not make haste slowly under such circumstances.   These are the ruins of a once fortified camp.

I wander about the flat top of the mountain and slowly there grows into recognizable form a great rectangle enclosed by large stones placed about two feet apart.   There is no doubt about the square and in one corner of it there seems an elevated mound covered with high-piled stones that would indicate a place for burials. *The fortified camp.* But not a trace of pottery or arrow-heads ; and about the stones only faint signs of fire which might have come from volcanic action as readily as from domestic hearths.   Upon the side of one of the large rocks are some characters in red ochre ; and on the ground near a pot-hole in the rock, something that the imagination might torture into a rude pestle for grinding maize.

The traces of human activity are slight.   Nature has been wearing them away and reclaiming her own on the mountain top.   Grease *Nature's reclamations.* wood is growing where once a floor was beaten hard as iron by human feet ; out of the burial mound rises a giant sahuaro whose branching arms give the look of the cross ; and beside the sahuaro rests a tall yucca with four feet of clustering bellflowers swinging from its top.

Mountain dwellers.

And who were they who built these stone walls, these primitive entrenchments ? When and where did they come from and what brought them here ? The hands that executed this rough work were certainly untrained. Indians ? Very likely. Perhaps some small band that had taken up a natural defence in the mountains because too feeble in numbers to fight in the open. Here from this lookout they could watch the country for a hundred miles around. Here the scouts could see far away the thin string of foemen winding snake-like over the ridges of the desert, could see them grow in size and count their numbers, could look down upon them at the foot of the mountain and yell back defiance to the challenge coming up the steep

Invading hosts.

sides. Brave indeed the invaders that would pluck the eagles from that eerie nest ! Climbing a hill against a shower of arrows, spears, and bowlders is to fight at a terrible disadvantage.

Starve them out ? Yes ; but the ones at the bottom would starve as quickly as those at the top. Cut off their water supply ? Yes ; but where did either besieged or besieger get water? *Water and food supplies.* If there was ever a spring in the mountain it long ago dried up, for there is no trace of it to-day. Possibly the mountain-dwellers knew of some arroyo where by digging in the sand they could get water. And possibly they carried it in ollas up the stone trail to their mountain home where they stored it in the rocks against the wrath of a siege to come. No doubt they took thought for trouble, and being native to the desert they could stand privation better than their enemies.

How long ago did that aboriginal band come *The aborigines.* trailing over these trackless deserts to find and make a home in a barren mountain standing in a bed of sand ? Who can tell ? A geologist might make the remains of their fort an illustration of the Stone Age and talk of unknown centuries ; an iconoclast might claim that it was merely a Mexican corral built to hide stolen horses ; but a plain person of the southwest would say that it was an old Indian camp. The builders of the fortification and the rectangle worked with stone because there was no other material. The man of the Stone Age exists to-day contemporary with civilized man. Possibly he always did. And it may be that some day Science will conclude that historic periods do not invariably happen, that there is not always a sequential evolution, and that the white race does not necessarily require a flat-headed mass of stupidity for an ancestor.

But what brought them to seek a dwelling place in the desert ? Were they driven out from the more fertile tracts ? Perhaps. Did they find this a country where game was plentiful and the conditions of life comparatively easy ? It is possible. Or was it that they loved the *The open desert.* open country, the hot sun, the treeless wastes, the great stretches of mesa, plain and valley ? Ah ; that is more than likely. Mankind has always loved the open plains. He is like an antelope and wishes to see about him in all directions. Perhaps, too, he was born with a predilection for "the view," but that is no easy matter to prove. It is sometimes assumed that humanity had naturally a sense and a feeling for the beautiful because the primitives decorated pottery and carved war-clubs and totem-posts. Again perhaps ; but from war-clubs and totem-posts to sunsets and mountain shadows *Perception of beauty.* —the love of the beautiful in nature—is a very long hark. The peons and Indians in Sonora cannot see the pinks and purples in the mountain shadows at sunset. They are astonished at your question for they see nothing but mountains. And you may vainly exhaust ingenuity trying to make a Pagago see the silvery sheen of the mesquite when the low sun is streaming across its tops. He sees only mesquite—the same dull mesquite through which he has chased rabbits from infancy.

No ; it is not likely that the tribe ever chose this abiding place for its scenery. A sensitive *Sense of beauty.* feeling for sound, or form, or color, an impressionable nervous organization, do not belong to the man with the hoe, much less to the man with the bow. It is to be feared that they are indicative of some physical degeneration, some decline in bone and muscle, some abnormal development of the emotional nature. They travel side by side with high civilization and are the premonitory symptoms of racial decay. But are we correct in assuming that because the red man does not see a colored shadow therefore he is blind to every charm and sublimity of nature ?

These mountain-dwellers, always looking out from their height, must have seen and re- *Mountain "view."* marked the large features of the desert—the great masses of form, the broad blocks of color.

They knew the long undulations of the valley-plain were covered with sharp, broken rock, but from this height surely they must have noticed how soft as velvet they looked, how smoothly they rolled from one into another, how perfectly they curved, how symmetrically they waved. And the long lines of the divides, lessening to the west—their ridges of grease wood showing a peculiar green like the crests of sea-waves in storm—did they not see them ? Did they not look down on the low neighboring hills and *The desert colors.* know that they were pink, terra-cotta, orange-colored—all the strange hues that may be compounded of clay and mineral—with here and there a crowning mass of white quartz or a far-extending outcrop of shale stained blue and green with copper ? Doubtless, a wealth of color and atmospheric effect was wasted upon the aboriginal retina ; but did it not take note of the deep orange sunsets, the golden fringed heaps of cumulus, and the tongues of fire that curled from every little cirrus cloud that lingered in the western sky ?

Looking down to the desert. And how often they must have looked out and down to the great basin of the desert where cloud and sky, mountain and mesa, seemed to dissolve into a pink mist ! It was not an unknown land to them and yet it had its terrors. Tradition told that the Evil Spirit dwelt there, and it was his hot breath that came up every morning on the wind, scorching and burning the brown faces of the mountain-dwellers! Fire!—he dwelt in fire. Whence came all the fierce glow of sunset down over that desert if it was not the reflection from his dwelling place? The very mountain peaks flared red at times, and in the old days there were rivers of fire. The petrified waves and eddies of those rivers were still visible in the lava streams. Were there not also great flames beneath the sands that threw up hot water and boiled great volcanoes of mud? And along the base of many a cliff were there not jets of steam and smoke blown out from the heart of the mountains? *The land of fire.*

It was a land of fire. No food, no grass, no water. There were places in the canyons where occasionally a little stream was found forcing itself up through the rock; but frequently it was salt or, worse yet, poisoned with copper or arsenic. How often the tribe had lost from its numbers—slain by the heat and drought in that waste! More than once the bodies had been found by crossing bands and always the same tale was told. The victims were half *Drought and heat.*

buried in sand, not decayed, but withered like the grass on the lomas.

Mystery—a mystery as luminous and yet as impenetrable as its own mirage—seemed always hanging over that low-lying waste. It was a vast pit dug under the mountain bases. The mountains themselves were bare crags of fire in the sunlight, and the sands of the pit grew only cactus and grease wood. There were tracts where nothing at all grew—miles upon miles of absolute waste with the pony's feet breaking through an alkaline crust. And again, there were dry lakes covered with silt ; and vast beds of sand and gypsum, white as snow and fine as dust. The pony's feet plunged in and came out leaving no trail. The surface smoothed over as though it were water. Fifty miles away one could see the desert sand-whirls moving slowly over the beds in tall columns two thousand feet high and shining like shafts of marble in the sunlight. How majestically they moved, their feet upon earth, their heads towering into the sky !

And then the desert winds that raised at times such furious clouds of sand ! All the air shone like gold dust and the sun turned red as blood. Ah ! what a stifling sulphureous

Desert mystery.

Sand and gypsum.

Sand-whirls.

air ! Even on the mountain tops that heavy air could be felt, and down in the desert itself the driving particles of sand cut the face and hands like blizzard-snow. The ponies could not be made to face it. They turned their backs to the wind and hung their heads between their fore feet. And how that wind roared and whistled through the thin grease wood ! The scrubby growths leaned and bent in the blast, the sand piled high on the trunks; and nothing but the enormous tap-roots kept them from being wrenched from the earth.

Desert storms.

And danger always followed the high winds. They blew the sands in clouds that drifted full and destroyed the trails. In a single night they would cover up a water hole, and in a few days fill in an arroyo where water could be got by digging. The sands drove like breakers on a beach, washing and wearing everything up to the bases of the mountains. And the fine sand reached still higher. It whirled up the canyons and across the saddles, it eddied around the enormous taluses, it even flung itself upon the face walls of the mountain and left the smoothing marks of its fingers upon the sharp pinnacles of the peak.

Drift of sand.

It was in winter when the winds were fiercest.

Winter cold. With them at times came a sharp cold, the more biting for the thin dry air of the desert. All the warmth seemed blown out of the basin with a breath, and its place filled by a storm-wind from the north that sent the condor wheeling down the blast and made the coyote shiver on the hill. How was it possible that such a furnace could grow so cold! And once or more each winter, when the sky darkened with clouds, there was a fall of snow that for an hour or so whitened the desert mountains and then passed away. At those times the springs were frozen, the high sierras were *Snow on desert.* snow-bound, and down in the desert it seemed as though a great frost-sheet had been let down from above. The brown skins for all their deer-hide clothing were red with cold, and the breath blown from the pony's nostrils was white as smoke.

A waste of intense heat and cold, of drouth and cloud-bursts, of winds and lightning, of storm and death, what could make any race of hunters or band of red men care for it? What was the attraction, wherein the fascination? *Sea and sand.* How often have we wondered why the sailor loves the sea, why the Bedouin loves the sand! What is there but a strip of sky and another

strip of sand or water ? But there is a simplicity about large masses — simplicity in
breadth, space and distance—that is inviting
and ennobling. And there is something very
restful about the horizontal line. Things that
lie flat are at peace and the mind grows peace-
ful with them. Furthermore, the waste places *Grim des-*
olation.
of the earth, the barren deserts, the tracts forsaken of men and given over to loneliness, have
a peculiar attraction of their own. The weird
solitude, the great silence, the grim desolation,
are the very things with which every desert
wanderer eventually falls in love. You think
that very strange perhaps ? Well, the beauty
of the ugly was sometime a paradox, but to-day
people admit its truth ; and the grandeur of
the desolate is just as paradoxical, yet the
desert gives it proof.

But the sun-tanned people who lived on this
mountain top never gave thought to masses,
or horizontal lines, or paradoxes. They lived
here, it may be from necessity at first, and then
stayed on because they loved the open wind- *Love for*
the desert.
blown country, the shining orange-hued sands,
the sweeping mesas, the great swing of the
horizontal circle, the flat desolation, the unbroken solitude. Nor ever knew why they

loved it. They were content and that was enough.

What finally became of them ? Who knows ? One by one they passed away, or perhaps were all slaughtered in a night by the fierce band newly come to numbers called the Apaches. This stone wall stands as their monument, but *The descent.* it tells no date or tale of death. As I descend the trail of stone the fancy keeps harping on the countless times the bare feet must have rubbed those blocks of syenite and porphyry to wear them so smooth. Have there been no others to clamber up these stairs of stone ? What of the Padres — were they not here ? As I ride off across the plain to the east the thought is of the heroism, the self-abnegation, the undying faith of those followers of Loyola and Xavier who came into this waste so many years ago. How idle seem all the specious *The Padres.* tales of Jesuitism and priestcraft. The Padres were men of soul, unshrinking faith, and a perseverance almost unparalleled in the annals of history. The accomplishments of Columbus, of Cortez, of Coronado were great ; but what of those who first ventured out upon these sands and erected missions almost in the heart of the desert, who single-handed coped with dangers from man and nature, and who lived and died without the slightest hope of reward here on earth ? Has not the sign of the cross cast more men in heroic mould than ever the glitter of the crown or the flash of the sword ?

And thinking such thoughts I turn to take a final view of the mountain ; and there on the fortified top something rears itself against the sky like the cross-hilt of a sword. It is the giant sahuaro with its rising arms, and beside it the cream-white bloom of the yucca shining in the sunlight seems like a lamp illuminating it. The good Padres have gone and their mission churches are crumbling back to the earth from which they were made ; but the light of *Light of the cross.* the cross still shines along the borders of this desert land. The flame, that through them the Spirit kindled, still burns ; and in every Indian village, in every Mexican adobe, you will see on the wall the wooden or grass-woven cross. On the high hills and at the cross-roads it stands, roughly hewn from mesquite and planted in a cone of stones. It is now always weather-stained and sun-cracked, but still the sign before which the peon and the Indian bow the head and whisper words of prayer. The dwellers beside the *Aboriginal faith.* desert have cherished what the inhabitants of the fertile plains have thrown away. They and their forefathers have never known civilization, and never suffered from the blight of doubt. Of a simple nature, they have lived in a simple way, close to their mother earth, beside the desert they loved, and (let us believe it !) nearer to the God they worshipped.

CHAPTER II

THE MAKE OF THE DESERT

THE first going - down into the desert is always something of a surprise. The fancy has pictured one thing; the reality shows quite another thing. Where and how did we gain the idea that the desert was merely a sea of *Sea of sand.* sand? Did it come from that geography of our youth with the illustration of the sand-storm, the flying camel, and the over-excited Bedouin? Or have we been reading strange tales told by travellers of perfervid imagination—the Marco Polos of to-day? There is, to be sure, some modicum of truth even in the statement that misleads. There are "seas" or lakes or ponds of sand on every desert; but they are not so vast, not so oceanic, that you ever lose sight of the land.

What land? Why, the mountains. The desert is traversed by many mountain ranges, *Mountain ranges on the desert.* some of them long, some short, some low, and some rising upward ten thousand feet. They are always circling you with a ragged horizon, dark-hued, bare-faced, barren—just as truly desert as the sands which were washed down from them. Between the ranges there are *Plains, val-* wide-expanding plains or valleys. The most *leys, and* arid portions of the desert lie in the basins of *mesas.* these great valleys—flat spaces that were once the beds of lakes, but are now dried out and left perhaps with an alkaline deposit that prevents vegetation. Through these valleys run arroyos or dry stream-beds—shallow channels where gravel and rocks are rolled during cloud-bursts and where sands drift with every wind. At times the valleys are more diversified, that is, broken by benches of land called mesas, dotted with small groups of hills called lomas, crossed by long stratified faces of rock called escarpments.

With these large features of landscape common to all countries, how does the desert differ from any other land ? Only in the matter of *Effect of* water—the lack of it. If Southern France *drought.* should receive no more than two inches of rain a year for twenty years it would, at the end of that time, look very like the Sahara, and the flashing Rhone would resemble the sluggish yellow Nile. If the Adirondack region in New

York were comparatively rainless for the same length of time we should have something like the Mojave Desert, with the Hudson changed into the red Colorado. The conformations of the lands are not widely different, but their surface appearances are as unlike as it is possible to imagine.

For the whole face of a land is changed by the rains. With them come meadow-grasses *The effect of rains.* and flowers, hillside vines and bushes, fields of yellow grain, orchards of pink-white blossoms. Along the mountain sides they grow the forests of blue-green pine, on the peaks they put white caps of snow ; and in the valleys they gather their waste waters into shining rivers and flashing lakes. This is the very sheen and sparkle —the witchery—of landscape which lend allurement to such countries as New England, France, or Austria, and make them livable and lovable lands.

But the desert has none of these charms. *Harshness of the desert.* Nor is it a livable place. There is not a thing about it that is "pretty," and not a spot upon it that is "picturesque" in any Berkshire-Valley sense. The shadows of foliage, the drift of clouds, the fall of rain upon leaves, the sound of running waters—all the gentler qualities of

nature that minor poets love to juggle with—
are missing on the desert. It is stern, harsh,
and at first repellent. But what tongue shall
tell the majesty of it, the eternal strength of it,
the poetry of its wide-spread chaos, the sublimity of its lonely desolation! And who shall
paint the splendor of its light; and from the
rising up of the sun to the going down of the
moon over the iron mountains, the glory of its

A gaunt land.

wondrous coloring! It is a gaunt land of
splintered peaks, torn valleys, and hot skies.
And at every step there is the suggestion of the
fierce, the defiant, the defensive. Everything
within its borders seems fighting to maintain
itself against destroying forces. There is a war
of elements and a struggle for existence going
on here that for ferocity is unparalleled elsewhere in nature.

The feeling of fierceness grows upon you as

Conditions of life.

you come to know the desert better. The sunshafts are falling in a burning shower upon
rock and dune, the winds blowing with the
breath of far-off fires are withering the bushes
and the grasses, the sands drifting higher and
higher are burying the trees and reaching up as
though they would overwhelm the mountains,
the cloud-bursts are rushing down the moun-

tain's side and through the torn arroyos as though they would wash the earth into the sea. The life, too, on the desert is peculiarly savage. *The incessant struggle.* It is a show of teeth in bush and beast and reptile. At every turn one feels the presence of the barb and thorn, the jaw and paw, the beak and talon, the sting and the poison thereof. Even the harmless Gila monster flattens his body on a rock and hisses a "Don't step on me." There is no living in concord or brotherhood here. Everything is at war with its neighbor, and the conflict is unceasing.

Yet this conflict is not so obvious on the face of things. You hear no clash or crash or snarl. *Elemental warfare.* The desert is overwhelmingly silent. There is not a sound to be heard; and not a thing moves save the wind and the sands. But you look up at the worn peaks and the jagged barrancas, you look down at the wash-outs and piled bowlders, you look about at the wind-tossed, half-starved bushes; and, for all the silence, you know that there is a struggle for life, a war for place, going on day by day.

How is it possible under such conditions for much vegetation to flourish? The grasses are *Desert vegetation.* scanty, the grease wood and cactus grow in patches, the mesquite crops out only along the

dry river-beds. All told there is hardly enough
covering to hide the anatomy of the earth.
And the winds are always blowing it aside.
You have noticed how bare and bony the hills
of New England are in winter when the trees
are leafless and the grasses are dead ? You have
seen the rocks loom up harsh and sharp, the
ledges assume angles, and the backbone and ribs
of the open field crop out of the soil ? The
desert is not unlike that all the year round.
To be sure there are snow-like driftings of sand
that muffle certain edges. Valleys, hills, and
even mountains are turned into rounded lines
by it at times. But the drift rolled high in
one place was cut out from some other place ;
and always there are *vertebræ* showing—elbows

Protruding edges.

and shoulders protruding through the yellow
byssus of sand.

The shifting sands ! Slowly they move, wave

Shifting sands.

upon wave, drift upon drift ; but by day and
by night they gather, gather, gather. They
overwhelm, they bury, they destroy, and then
a spirit of restlessness seizes them and they
move off elsewhere, swirl upon swirl, line upon
line, in serpentine windings that enfold some
new growth or fill in some new valley in the
waste. So it happens that the surface of the

desert is far from being a permanent affair. There is hardly enough vegetation to hold the sands in place. With little or no restraint upon them they are transported hither and yon at the mercy of the winds.

Yet the desert winds hardly blow where they list. They follow certain channels or "draws" through the mountain ranges; and the reason for their doing so is plain enough. During the day the intense heat of the desert, meeting with only a thin dry air above it, rises rapidly skyward leaving a vast vacuum below that must be filled with a colder air from without. This colder air on the southern portion of the Colorado Desert comes in from the Gulf region. One can feel it in the passes of the mountains about Baboquivari, rushing up toward the heated portions of Arizona around Tucson. And the hotter the day the stronger the inward rush of the wind. Some days it will blow at the rate of fifty miles an hour until sunset, and then with a cessation of radiation the wind stops and the night is still.

Desert winds.

Radiation of heat.

On the western portions of the Colorado the wind comes from the Pacific across Southern California. The hot air from the desert goes up and out over the Coast Range, reaching sea-

ward. How far out it goes is unknown, but
when it has cooled off it descends and flows
back toward the land as the daily sea-breeze.
It re-enters the desert through such loop holes

in the Coast Range as the San Gorgonio Pass—
the old Puerta de San Carlos—above Indio.
The rush of it through that pass is quite violent at times.   For wind is very much like
water and seeks the least obstructed way.   Its
goal is usually the hottest and the lowest place
on the desert—such a place, for example, as
Salton, though I am not prepared to point out
the exact spot on the desert that the winds
choose as a target.   On the Mojave Desert at
the north their action is similar, though there
they draw down from the Mount Whitney region as well as from the Pacific.

In open places these desert winds are sometimes terrific in force though usually they are
moderate and blow with steadiness from certain
directions.   As you feel them softly blowing

against your cheek it is hard to imagine that they
have any sharp edge to them.   Yet about you
on every side is abundant evidence of their
works.   The sculptor's sand-blast works swifter
but not surer.   Granite and porphyry cannot
withstand them, and in time they even cut

through the glassy surface of lava. Their wear is not here nor there, but all over, everywhere. The edge of the wind is always against the stone. Continually there is the slow erosion of canyon, crag, and peak; forever there is a gnawing at the bases and along the face-walls of the great sierras. Grain by grain, the vast foundations, the beetling escarpments, the high domes in air are crumbled away and drifted into the valleys. *Erosion of mountains.* Nature heaved up these mountains at one time to fulfil a purpose: she is now taking them down to fulfil another purpose. If she has not water to work with here as elsewhere she is not baffled of her purpose. Wind and sand answer quite as well.

But the cutting of the wind is not always even or uniform, owing to the inequalities in the fibre of rock; and often odd effects are produced by the softer pieces of rock wearing away first and leaving the harder section exposed to view. Frequently these remainders take on fantastic shapes and are likened to things human, such as faces, heads, and hands. In the San Gorgonio Pass the rock-cuttings are in *Rock-cutting.* parallel lines, and occasionally a row of garnets in the rock will make the jewel-pointed fingers of a hand protruding from the parent body.* Again shafts of hard granite may make tall spires and turrets upon a mountain peak, a vein of quartz may bulge out in a white or yellow or rose-colored band ; and a ridge of black lava, reaching down the side of a foot-hill, may creep and heave like the backbone of an enormous dragon.

Fantastic forms.

Perhaps the greatest erosion is in the passes through which the winds rush into the desert. Here they not only eat into the ledges and cut away the rock faces, but they make great wash-outs in the desert itself. These trenches look in every respect as though caused by water. In fact the effects of wind and water are often so inextricably mixed that not even an expert geologist would be able to say where the one leaves off and the other begins. The shallow caves of the mountains—too high up for any wave action from sea or lake, and too deep to be reached by rains—have all the rounded appearance of water-worn receptacles. One can almost see the water-lines upon the walls. But the sand-heaped floor suggests that the agent of erosion was the wind.

Wash-outs.

Sand-lines in caves.

Yes ; there is some water on the deserts, some

* Professor Blake of the University of Arizona has called my attention to this.

rainfall each year. Even Sahara gets its occasional showers, and the Colorado and the Mojave show many traces of the cloud-burst. The *Cloud-bursts.* dark thunder-clouds that occasionally gather over the desert seem at times to reserve all their stores of rain for one place. The fall is usually short-lived but violent; and its greatest force is always on the mountains. There is no sod, no moss, to check or retard the flood; and the result is a great rush of water to the low places. In the canyons the swollen streams roll down *Canyon streams.* bowlders that weigh tons, and in the ravines many a huge barranca is formed in a single hour by these rushing waters. On the lomas and sloping valleys they are not less destructive, running in swift streams down the hollows, and whirling stones, sand, and torn bushes into the old river-beds.

In a very short time there is a great torrent pouring down the valley—a torrent composed of water, sand, and gravel in about equal parts. It is a yellow, thick stream that has nothing but disaster for the man or beast that seeks to swim *Desert floods.* it. Many a life has been lost there. The great onset of the water destroys anything like buoyancy, and the tendency is to drag down and roll the swimmer like a bowlder. Even the enormous strength of the grizzly bear has been known to fail him in these desert rivers. They boil and seethe as though they were hot; and they rush on against banks, ripping out the *Power of water.* long roots of mesquite, and swirling away tons of undermined gravel as though it were only so much snow. At last after miles of this mill-racing the force begins to diminish, the streams reach the flat lake-beds and spread into broad, thin sheets; and soon they have totally vanished, leaving scarce a rack behind.

The desert rainfall comes quickly and goes quickly. The sands drink it up, and it sinks to the rock strata, where, following the ledges, it is finally shelved into some gravel-bed. There, perhaps a hundred feet under the sand, it slow-*Water-pockets.* ly oozes away to the river or the Gulf. There is none of it remains upon the surface except perhaps a pool caught in a clay basin, or a catch of water in a rocky bowl of some canyon. Occasionally one meets with a little stream where a fissure in the rock and a pressure from below forces up some of the water; but these *No running streams.* springs are of very rare occurrence. And they always seem a little strange. A brook that ran on the top of the ground would be an anomaly here; and after one lives many months on the desert and returns to a well-watered country, the last thing he becomes accustomed to is the sight of running water.

In every desert there are isolated places where water stands in pools, fed by underground springs, where mesquite and palms grow, and where there is a show of coarse grass over some acres. These are the so-called oases in the waste that travellers have pictured *Oases in the waste.* as Gardens of Paradise, and poets have used for centuries as illustrations of happiness surrounded by despair. To tell the truth they are wretched little mud-holes; and yet because of their few trees and their pockets of yellow brackish water they have an appearance of unreality. They are strange because bright-green foliage and moisture of any kind seem out of place on the desert.

Yet surely there was plenty of water here at one time. Everywhere you meet with the dry lake-bed—its flat surface devoid of life and often glimmering white with salt. These beds are no doubt of recent origin geologically, and were never more than the catch-basins of sur- *Catch-basins.* face water; but long before ever they were brought forth the whole area of the desert was under the sea. To-day one may find on the high table-lands sea-shells in abundance. The petrified clams are precisely like the live clams that one picks up on the western coast of Mexico. The corals, barnacles, dried sponge forms, and cellular rocks do not differ from those in the Gulf of California. The change *Old sea-beds.* from sea to shore, and from shore to table-land and mountain, no doubt took place very slowly. Just how many centuries ago who shall say ? Geologists may guess and laymen may doubt, but the Keeper of the Seals says nothing.

Nor is it known just when the porphyry mountains were roasted to a dark wine-red, and the foot-hills burnt to a terra-cotta orange. Fire has been at work here as well as wind *Volcanic action.* and water. The whole country has a burnt and scorched look proceeding from something more fiery than sunlight. Volcanoes have left their traces everywhere. You can still see the streams of lava that have chilled as they ran. The blackened cones with their craters exist ; and about them, for many miles, there are *Lava streams.* great lakes and streams of reddish-black lava, frozen in swirls and pools, cracked like glass, broken into blocks like a ruined pavement. Wherever you go on the desert you meet with chips and breaks of lava, showing that at one time there must have been quantities of it belched out of the volcanoes.

There were convulsions in those days when the sea washed close to the bases of the mountains. Through the crevasses and fissures in the rocks the water crept into the fires of the earth, and explosions—volcanic eruptions—were the result. Wandering over these stony tracks you might fancy that all strata and all geological ages were blown into discord by those explosions. For here are many kinds of splintered and twisted rocks—rocks aqueous and igneous, gritstones, conglomerates, shales, slates, syenite, basalt. And everywhere the white coatings of carbonate of lime that look as though they were run hot from a puddling furnace; and the dust of sulphur, copper, and iron blown upon granite as though oxidized by fire. *Geological ages.*

Kinds of rock.

The evidence for glaciers is not so convincing. There is no apparent sign of an ice age. Occasionally one sees scratches upon mountain walls that are suspicious, or heaps of sand and gravel that look as though pushed into the small valleys by some huge force. And again there are places on the Mojave where windrows *Glaciers.*

of heavy bowlders are piled on either side of mountain water-courses, looking as though ice may have caused their peculiar placing. But *Land slips.* there is no certainty about any of these. Land slips may have made the windrows as easily as ice slips ; and water can heap mounds of sand and gravel as readily as glaciers. One cannot trace the geological ages with such facility. Things sometimes "just happen," in spite of scientific theories.

Movement of stones. Besides, the movement of the stones into the valleys is going on continuously, irrespective of glaciers. They are first broken from the peaks by erosion, and then they fall into what is called *The talus.* a talus—a great slope of stone blocks beginning half way down the mountain and often reaching to the base or foot. Many of them, of course, are rolled over steep declivities into the canyons and thence carried down by flood waters ; but the talus is the more uniform method for bowlders reaching the plain.

In the first stage of the talus the blocks are ragged-edged and as large as a barrel. Nothing whatever grows upon the slope. It is as bare as the side of a volcanic crater. And just as difficult to walk over. The talus is added to at the top by the falling rock of the face-wall, and it is losing at the bottom by the under blocks grinding away to stone and gravel. The flattening out at the bottom, the breaking up of the blocks, and the push-out of the mountain foot upon the plain is the second stage of the talus. In almost all the large valleys of the desert the depressed talus extends, sometimes miles in length, out from the foot of the mountain range. When it finally slips down into the valley and becomes a flat floor it has entered upon its third and last stage. It is then the ordinary valley-bed covered with its cactus and cut by its arroyos. Yet this valley-floor instead of being just one thing is really many things— or rather made up of many different materials and showing many different surfaces. *Stages of the talus.*

You may spend days and weeks studying the make-up of these desert-floors. Beyond Yuma on the Colorado there are thousands of acres of mosaic pavement, made from tiny blocks of jasper, carnelian, agate—a pavement of pebbles so hard that a horse's hoof will make no impression upon it—wind-swept, clean, compact as though pressed down by a roller. One can imagine it made by the winds that have cut and drifted away the light sands and allowed the pebbles to settle close together until they *Desert-floors.*

have become wedged in a solid surface. For no known reason other portions of the desert are

covered with blocks of red-incrusted sandstone —the incrustation being only above the sand-line. In the lake-beds there is usually a surface of fine silt. It is not a hard surface though it often has a crust upon it that a wildcat can walk upon, but a horse or a man would pound through as easily as through crusted snow.

The salt-beds are of sporadic appearance and hardly count as normal features of the desert. They are often quite beautiful in appearance. The one on the Colorado near Salton is hard as ice, white, and after sunset it often turns blue, yellow, or crimson, dependent upon the sky overhead which it reflects. Borax and gypsum-beds are even scarcer than the salt-beds. They are also white and often very brilliant reflectors

of the sky. The sand-beds are, of course, more frequently met with than any others ; and yet your horse does not go knee-deep in sand for any great distance. It is too light, and is drifted too easily by the winds. Bowlders, gravel, and general mountain wash is the most common flooring of all.

The mountains whence all the wash comes, are mere ranges of rock. In the canyons, where there is perhaps some underground water, there are occasionally found trees and large bushes, and the very high sierras have forests of pine belted about their tops ; but usually the desert ranges are barren. They never bore fruit. The washings from them are grit and fry of rock but no vegetable mould. The black dirt that lies a foot or more in depth upon the surface of the eastern prairies, showing the many years accumulations of decayed grasses and weeds, is not known anywhere on the desert. The slight vegetation that grows never has a chance to turn into mould. And besides, nothing ever rots or decays in these sands. Iron will not rust, nor tin tarnish, nor flesh mortify. The grass and the shrub wither and are finally cut into pieces by flying sands. Sometimes you may see small particles of grass or twigs heaped about an ant-hill, or find them a part of a bird's nest in a cholla ; but usually they turn to dry dust and blow with the wind—at the wind's will.

Mountain vegetation.

Withered grasses.

The desert mountains gathered in clusters along the waste, how old and wrinkled, how set and determined they look ! Somehow they remind you of a clinched hand with the knuckles turned skyward. They have strength and bulk, the suggestion of quiescent force.

Barren rock.

Barren rock and nothing more ; but what could better epitomize power ! The heave of the enormous ridge, the loom of the domed top, the bulk and body of the whole are colossal. Rising as they do from flat sands they give the impression of things deep-based—veritable islands of porphyry bent upward from a yellow

Mountain colors.

sea. They are so weather-stained, so worn, that they are not bright in coloring. Usually they assume a dull garnet-red, or the red of peroxide of iron ; but occasionally at sunset they warm in color and look fire-red through the pink haze.

The more abrupt ranges that appear younger

Saw-toothed ridges.

because of their saw-toothed ridges and broken peaks, are often much finer in coloring. They have needles that are lifted skyward like Moslem minarets or cathedral spires ; and at evening, if there is a yellow light, they shine like brazen spear-points set against the sky. It is astonishing that dull rock can disclose such marvellous coloring. The coloring is not local in the rock, nor yet again entirely reflected. Desert atmosphere, with which we shall have to reckon hereafter, has much to do with it.

And whether at sunset, at sunrise, or at midnight, how like watch-towers these mountains stand above the waste! One can almost fancy that behind each dome and rampart there are cloud-like Genii—spirits of the desert—keeping guard over this kingdom of the sun. And what a far-reaching kingdom they watch! Plain upon plain leads up and out to the horizon—far as the eye can see—in undulations of gray and gold; ridge upon ridge melts into the blue of the distant sky in lines of lilac and purple; fold upon fold over the mesas the hot air drops its veilings of opal and topaz. Yes; it is the kingdom of sun-fire. For every color in the scale is attuned to the key of flame, every air-wave comes with the breath of flame, every sunbeam falls as a shaft of flame. There is no questioning who is sovereign in these dominions.

Seen from the peaks.

Sun-fire kingdom.

CHAPTER III

THE BOTTOM OF THE BOWL

Early geological days.

IN the ancient days when the shore of the Pacific was young, when the white sierras had only recently been heaved upward and the desert itself was in a formative stage, the ocean reached much farther inland than at the present time. It pushed through many a pass and flooded many a depression in the sands, as its wave-marks upon granite bases and its numerous beaches still bear witness. In those days that portion of the Colorado Desert known as the Salton Basin did not exist. The Gulf of California extended as far north as the San Bernardino Range and as far west as the Pass of San Gorgonio. Its waters stood deep where now lies the road-bed of the Southern Pacific railway, and all the country from Indio almost to the Colorado River was a blue sea. The Bowl was full. No one knew if it had a bottom or imagined that it would ever be emptied of water and given over to the drifting sands.

The former Gulf.

44

No doubt the tenure of the sea in this Salton Basin was of long duration. The sand-dunes still standing along the northern shore—fifty feet high and shining like hills of chalk—were not made in a month ; nor was the long shelving beach beneath them — still covered with sea-shells and pebbles and looking as though washed by the waves only yesterday—formed in a day. Both dunes and beach are plainly visible winding across the desert for many miles. The southwestern shore, stretching under a spur of the Coast Range, shows the same formation in its beach-line. The old bays and lagoons that led inland from the sea, the river-beds that brought down the surface waters from the mountains, the inlets and natural harbors are all in place. Some of them are drifted half full of sand, but they have not lost their identity. And out in the sea-bed still stand masses of cellular rock, honeycombed and water-worn (and now for many years wind-worn), showing the places where once rose the reefs of the ancient sea.

Sea-beaches on desert.

Harbors and reefs.

These are the only records that tell of the sea's occupation. The Indians have no tradition about it. Yet when the sea was there the Indian tribes were there also. Along the

Indian remains.

bases of the San Bernardino and San Jacinto Ranges there are indications of cave-dwelling, rock-built squares that doubtless were fortified camps, heaps of stone that might have been burial-mounds. Everywhere along the ancient shores and beaches you pick up pieces of pottery, broken ollas, stone pestels and mortars, axe‐heads, obsidian arrow‐heads, flint spear-points, agate beads. There is not the slightest doubt that the shores were inhabited. It was a warm nook, accessible to the mountains and the Pacific; in fact, just the place where tribes would naturally gather. Branches of

The Cocopas.

the Yuma Indians, like the Cocopas, overran all this country when the Padres first crossed the desert; and it was probably their fore-fathers who lived by the shores of this Upper Gulf. No doubt they were fishermen, traders and fighters, like their modern representatives on Tiburon Island; and no doubt they fished and fought and were happy by the shores of the mountain-locked sea.

But there came a time when there was a disturbance of the existing conditions in the Up-

The Colorado River.

per Gulf. Century after century the Colorado River had been carrying down to the sea its burden of sedimental sand and silt. It had been entering the Gulf far down on the eastern side at an acute angle. Gradually its deposits had been building up, banking up ; and gradually the river had been pushing them out and across the Gulf in a southwesterly direction. Finally there was formed a delta dam stretching from shore to shore. The tides no longer brought water up and around the bases of the big mountains. Communication with the sea was cut off and what was once the top of the Gulf changed into an inland lake. It now had no water supply from below, it lay under a burning sun, and day by day evaporation carried it away.

The delta dam.

No one knows how many days, how many years, elapsed before the decrease of the water became noticeable. Doubtless the lake shrunk away slowly from the white face of the sand-dunes and the red walls of the mountains. The river-mouths that opened into the lake narrowed themselves to small stream - beds. The shelving beaches where the waves had fallen lazily year after year, pushing themselves over the sand in beautiful water-mirrors, shone bare and dry in the sunlight. The ragged reefs, over which the chop sea had tumbled and tossed so long, lifted their black hulks out

The inland lake.

of the water and with their hosts of barnacles and sea-life became a part of the land.

The first fall.

The waters of the great inland lake fell perhaps a hundred feet and then they made a pause. The exposed shores dried out. They baked hard in the sun, and were slowly ground down to sand and powdered silt by the action of the winds. The waters made a long pause. They were receiving reinforcements from some source. Possibly there was more rainfall in those days than now, and the streams entering the lake from the mountains were much larger. Again there

Springs and wells in the sea-bed.

may have been underground springs. There are flowing wells to-day in this old sea-bed— wells that cast up water salter than the sea itself. No one knows their fountain-head. Perhaps by underground channels the water creeps through from the Gulf, or comes from mountain reservoirs and turns saline by passing through beds of salt. These are the might-bes ; but it is far more probable that the Colorado River at high water had made a breach of some kind in the dam of its own construction and had poured overflow water into the lake by way of a dry

The New River.

channel called the New River. The bed of this river runs northward from below the boundary-line of Lower California ; and in 1893, during a rise in the Colorado, the waters rushed in and flooded the whole of what is called the Salton Basin. When the Colorado receded, the basin soon dried out again.

It was undoubtedly some accident of this kind that called the halt in the original recession. During the interim the lake had time to form new shores where the waves pounded and washed on the gravel as before until miles upon miles of new beach—pebbled, shelled, and sloping downward with great uniformity—came into existence. This secondary beach is intact to-day and looks precisely like the primary except that it is not quite so large. Across the basin, along the southern mountains, the second water-tracery is almost as apparent as the first. The rocks are eaten in long lines by wave-action, and are honeycombed by the ceaseless energies of the zoöphite. *New beaches.*

Nor was the change in beach and rock alone. New bays and harbors were cut out from where the sea had been, new river - channels were opened down to the shrunken lake, new lagoons were spread over the flat places. Nature evidently made a great effort to repair the damage and adapt the lake to its new conditions. And the Indians, too, accepted the change. There *The second fall.*

are many indications in broken pottery, arrow-heads, and mortars that the aboriginal tribes moved down to the new beach and built wick-iups by the diminished waters. And the old fishing-foraging-fighting life was probably re-sumed.

Then once more the waters went down, down, down. Step by step they receded until the sec-ondary beach was left a hundred feet above the water level. Again there was a pause. Again *The third beach.* new beaches were beaten into shape by the waves, new bays were opened, new arroyos cut through from above. The whole process of shore-making—the fitting of the land to the shrunken proportions of the lake — was gone through with for the third time ; while the water supply from the river or elsewhere was maintained in decreased volume but with some steadiness of flow. Possibly the third halt of the receding water was not for a great length of time. The tertiary beach is not so large as its predecessors. There never was any strong wave-*The failing water.* action upon it, its pebbles are few, its faults and breaks are many. The water supply was failing, and finally it ceased altogether.

What fate for a lake in the desert receiving no supplies from river or sea—what fate save

annihilation ?   The hot breath of the wind blew
across the cramped water and whipped its surface into little waves; and as each tiny point
of spray rose on the crest and was lifted into
the air the fiery sunbeam caught it, and in a
twinkling had evaporated and carried it up- *Evapo-*
ward.   Day by day this process went on over *ration.*
the whole surface until there was no more sea.
The hollow reefs rose high and dark above the
bed, the flat shoals of silt lifted out of the ooze,
and down in the lowest pools there was the
rush and plunge of monster tortuabas, sharks
and porpoises, caught as it were in a net and
vainly struggling to get out.   How strange must
have seemed that landscape when the low ridges
were shining with the slime of the sea, when
the beds were strewn with *algæ*, sponges, and
coral, and the shores were whitening with salt !
How strange, indeed, must have been the first
sight of the Bottom of the Bowl!   *Bottom of*
                                                   the Bowl.
But the sun never relaxed its fierce heat nor
the wind its hot breath.   They scorched and
burned the silt of the sea-bed until it baked *Drying out*
and cracked into blocks.   Then began the wear *of the sea-*
of the winds upon the broken edges until the *bed.*
blocks were reduced to dry fine powder.   Finally the desert came in.   Drifts upon drifts of

sand blown through the valleys settled in the empty basin; gravel and bowlder-wash came down from the mountains; the grease wood, the salt-bush, and the so-called pepper-grass sprang up in isolated spots. Slowly the desert fastened itself upon the basin. Its heat became *Advance of desert.* too intense to allow the falling rain to reach the earth, its surface was too salt and alkaline to allow of much vegetation, it could support neither animal nor bird life; it became more deserted than the desert itself.

And thus it remains to this day. When you are in the bottom of it you are nearly three *Below sea-level.* hundred feet below the level of the sea. Circling about you to the north, south, and west are sierras, some of them over ten thousand feet in height. These form the Rim of the Bowl. And off to the southwest there is a side broken out of the Bowl through which you can pass to the river and the Gulf. The basin is perhaps the hottest place to be found anywhere on the *Desolation of the basin.* American deserts. And it is also the most forsaken. The bottom itself is, for the great part of it, as flat as a table. It looks like a great plain leading up and out to the horizon—a plain that has been ploughed and rolled smooth. The soil is drifted silt—the deposits made by the washings from the mountains — and is almost as fine as flour.

The long line of dunes at the north are just as desolate, yet they are wonderfully beautiful. *Beauty of the sand-dunes.* The desert sand is finer than snow, and its curves and arches, as it builds its succession of drifts out and over an arroyo, are as graceful as the lines of running water. The dunes are always rhythmical and flowing in their forms; and for color the desert has nothing that surpasses them. In the early morning, before the sun is up, they are air-blue, reflecting the sky overhead; at noon they are pale lines of dazzling orange-colored light, waving and undulating in the heated air ; at sunset they are often flooded with a rose or mauve color ; under a blue moonlight they shine white as icebergs in the northern seas.

But neither the dunes nor the flats grow vegetation of consequence. About the high edges, up near the mountain slopes, you find growths of mesquite, palo verde, and cactus ; *Cactus and salt-bush.* but down in the basin there are many miles where no weed or grass breaks the level uniformity. Not even the salt-bush will grow in some of the areas. And this is not due to poverty of soil but to absence of water and intense heat.   Plants cannot live by sunlight alone.

Desert animals in the basin.

Nor will the desert animals inhabit an absolute waste. The coyote and the wildcat do not relish life in this dip in the earth.   They care little for heat and drouth, but the question of food appeals to them.   There is nothing to eat. Even the abstemious jack-rabbit finds living here something of a difficulty.   Many kinds of tracks are found in the uncrusted silt—tracks of coyotes, gray wolves, sometimes mountain lions—but they all run in straight trails, showing the animals to be crossing the basin to the mountains, not prowling or hunting. So, too,

Birds.

you will occasionally find birds—linnets, bobolinks, mocking-birds, larks—but they are seen one at a time, and they look weary-like land birds far out at sea that seek a resting-place on passing vessels.   They do not belong to the desert and are only stopping there temporarily

Lizards and snakes.

on some long flight. Snakes and lizards are not particular about their abiding-place, and yet they do not care to live in a land where there is no bush or stone to creep under.   You meet with them very seldom.   Practically there is no life of any kind that is native to the place.

Is there any beauty, other than the dunes,

down in this hollow of the desert? Yes.
From a picturesque point of view it has the
most wonderful light, air, and color imaginable.
You will not think so until you see them
blended in that strange illusion known as
mirage. And here is the one place in all the *Mirage.*
world where the water-mirage appears to perfection. It does not show well over grassy or
bushy ground, but over the flat lake-beds of the
desert its appearance is astonishing. Down in
the basin it is accompanied by a second illusion *The water
illusion.*
that makes the first more convincing. You
are below sea-level, but instead of the ground
about you sloping up and out, it apparently
slopes down and away on every side. You are
in the centre of a disk or high point of ground,
and around the circumference of the disk is
water—palpable, almost tangible, water. It
cannot be seen well from your horse, and fifty
feet up on a mountain side it would not be
visible at all. But dismount and you see it
better ; kneel down and place your cheek to the
ground and now the water seems to creep up to
you. You could throw a stone into it. The
shore where the waves lap is just before you.
But where is the horizon-line ? Odd enough,
this vast circling sea does not always know a

horizon ; it sometimes reaches up and blends
into the sky without any point of demarcation.
Through the heated air you see faint outlines of
mountains, dim glimpses of foot-hills, suggestions of distance ; but no more.   Across them
is drawn the wavering veil of air, and the red
earth at your feet, the blue sky overhead, are
but bordering bands of flat color.

Decorative landscapes.   And there you have the most decorative landscape in the world, a landscape all color, a dream
landscape.   Painters for years have been trying
to put it upon canvas—this landscape of color,
light, and air, with form almost obliterated,
merely suggested, given only as a hint of the
mysterious.   Men like Corot and Monet have
told us, again and again, that in painting, clearly
delineated forms of mountains, valleys, trees,
and rivers, kill the fine color-sentiment of the
picture.   The great struggle of the modern
landscapist is to get on with the least possible
form and to suggest everything by tones of color,
shades of light, drifts of air.   Why ?   Because
Sensuous qualities in nature.   these are the most sensuous qualities in nature
and in art.   The landscape that is the simplest
in form and the finest in color is by all odds the
most beautiful.   It is owing to just these features that this Bowl of the desert is a thing of

beauty instead of a dreary hollow in the hills.
Only one other scene is comparable to it, and
that the southern seas at sunset when the calm
ocean reflects and melts into the color-glory of
the sky. It is the same kind of beauty. Form
is almost blurred out in favor of color and air.

Yet here is more beauty destined to destruction. It might be thought that this forsaken
pot-hole in the ground would never come under
the dominion of man, that its very worthlessness
would be its safeguard against civilization, that
none would want it, and everyone from necessity
would let it alone. But not even the spot deserted by reptiles shall escape the industry or the
avarice (as you please) of man. A great company
has been formed to turn the Colorado River
into the sands, to reclaim this desert basin, and
make it blossom as the rose. The water is to
be brought down to the basin by the old channel
of the New River. Once in reservoirs it is to be
distributed over the tract by irrigating ditches,
and it is said a million acres of desert will thus
be made arable, fitted for homesteads, ready for
the settler who never remains settled.

A most laudable enterprise, people will say.
Yes; commercially no one can find fault with
it. Money made from sand is likely to be clean

*Changing
the desert.*

*Irrigation
in the basin.*

Changing
the climate.
money, at any rate. And economically these acres will produce large supplies of food. That is commendable, too, even if those for whom it is produced waste a good half of what they already possess. And yet the food that is produced there may prove expensive to people other than the producers. This old sea-bed is, for its area, probably the greatest dry-heat generator in the world because of its depression and its barren, sandy surface. It is a furnace that whirls heat up and out of the Bowl, over the peaks of the Coast Range into Southern California, and eastward across the plains to Arizona and Sonora. In what measure it is responsible for the general climate of those States cannot be accurately summarized ; but it certainly has a great influence, especially in the
Dry air.
matter of producing dry air. To turn this desert into an agricultural tract would be to increase humidity, and that would be practically to nullify the finest air on the continent.

And why are not good air and climate as essential to human well-being as good beef and good bread ? Just now, when it is a world too late, our Government and the forestry societies of the country are awakening to the necessity of preserving the forests. National parks are being created wherever possible and the cutting of timber within them is prohibited. Why is this being done? Ostensibly to preserve the trees, but in reality to preserve the water supply, to keep the fountain-heads pure, to maintain a uniform stage of water in the rivers. Very proper and right. The only pity is that it was not undertaken forty years ago. But how is the water supply, from an economic and hygienic stand-point, any more important than the air supply?

Value of the air supply.

Grasses, trees, shrubs, growing grain, they, too, may need good air as well as human lungs. The deserts are not worthless wastes. You cannot crop all creation with wheat and alfalfa. Some sections must lie fallow that other sections may produce. Who shall say that the preternatural productiveness of California is not due to the warm air of its surrounding deserts? Does anyone doubt that the healthfulness of the countries lying west of the Mississippi may be traced directly to the dry air and heat of the deserts. They furnish health to the human; why not strength to the plant? The deserts should never be reclaimed. They are the breathing-spaces of the west and should be preserved forever.

Value of the deserts.

To speak about sparing anything because it is beautiful is to waste one's breath and incur ridicule in the bargain. The æsthetic sense—the power to enjoy through the eye, the ear, and the imagination—is just as important a factor in the scheme of human happiness as the corporeal sense of eating and drinking ; but there has never been a time when the world would admit it. The "practical men," who seem forever on the throne, know very well that beauty is only meant for lovers and young persons — stuff to suckle fools withal. The main affair of life is to get the dollar, and if there is any money in cutting the throat of Beauty, why, by all means, cut her throat. That is what the "practical men" have been doing ever since the world began. It is not necessary to dig up ancient history ; for have we not seen, here in California and Oregon, in our own time, the destruction of the fairest valleys the sun ever shone upon by placer and hydraulic mining ? Have we not seen in Minnesota and Wisconsin the mightiest forests that ever raised head to the sky slashed to pieces by the axe and turned into a waste of tree-stumps and fallen timber ? Have we not seen the Upper Mississippi, by the destruction of

Destruction of natural beauty.

Effects of mining, lumbering, agriculture.

the forests, changed from a broad, majestic
river into a shallow, muddy stream; and the
beautiful prairies of Dakota turned under by *Ploughing the prairies.*
the plough and then allowed to run to weeds?
Men must have coal though they ruin the valleys and blacken the streams of Pennsylvania,
they must have oil though they disfigure half
of Ohio and Indiana, they must have copper
if they wreck all the mountains of Montana
and Arizona, and they must have gold though
they blow Alaska into the Behring Sea. It is
more than possible that the "practical men" *"Practical men"*
have gained much practice and many dol-
lars by flaying the fair face of these United
States. They have stripped the land of its
robes of beauty, and what have they given in
its place? Weeds, wire fences, oil-derricks,
board shanties and board towns—things that
not even a "practical man" can do less than
curse at.

And at last they have turned to the desert!
It remains to be seen what they will do with it.
Reclaiming a waste may not be so easy as breaking a prairie or cutting down a forest. And
Nature will not always be driven from her
purpose. Wind, sand, and heat on Sahara *Fighting wind, sand, and heat.*
have proven hard forces to fight against; they

may prove no less potent on the Colorado. And sooner or later Nature will surely come to her own again. Nothing human is of long duration. Men and their deeds are obliterated, *Nature eternal.* the race itself fades; but Nature goes calmly on with her projects. She works not for man's enjoyment, but for her own satisfaction and her own glory. She made the fat lands of the earth with all their fruits and flowers and foliage; and with no less care she made the desert with its sands and cacti. She intended that each should remain as she made it. When the locust swarm has passed, the flowers and grasses will return to the valley; when man is gone, the sand and the heat will come back *Return of desolation.* to the desert. The desolation of the kingdom will live again, and down in the Bottom of the Bowl the opalescent mirage will waver skyward on wings of light, serene in its solitude, though no human eye sees nor human tongue speaks its loveliness.

CHAPTER IV

THE SILENT RIVER

THE career of the Colorado, from its rise in the Wind River Mountains in Wyoming to its final disappearance in the Gulf of California, seems almost tragic in its swift transitions. It starts out so cheerily upon its course ; it is so clear and pure, so sparkling with sunshine and spirit. It dashes down mountain valleys, gurgles under bowlders, swirls over waterfalls, flashes through ravines and gorges. With its sweep and glide and its silvery laugh it seems to lead a merry life. But too soon it plunges into precipitous canyons and enters upon its fierce struggle with the encompassing rock. Now it boils and foams, leaps and strikes, thunders and shatters. For hundreds of miles it wears and worries and undermines the rock to its destruction. During the long centuries it has cut down into the crust of the earth five thousand feet. But ever the stout walls keep casting it back, keep churning it into bubbles, beating it

Rise of the Colorado.

In the canyon.

63

into froth. At last, its canyon course run, exhausted and helpless, it is pushed through the escarpments, thrust out upon the desert, to find its way to the sea as best it can. Its spirit is broken, its vivacity is extinguished, its color is deepened to a dark red—the trail of blood that leads up to the death. Wearily now it drifts across the desert without a ripple, without a moan. Like a wounded snake it drags its length far down the long wastes of sand to where the blue waves are flashing on the Californian Gulf. And there it meets—obliteration.

On the desert.

After the clash and roar of the conflict in the canyons how impressive seems the stillness of the desert, how appalling the unbroken silence of the lower river ! Day after day it moves seaward, but without a sound. You start at its banks to find no waves, no wash upon gravel beaches, no rush of water over shoals. Instead of the soothing murmur of breaking falls there is at times the boil of currents from below— waters flung up sullenly and soon flattened into drifting nothingness by their own weight.

The lower river.

And how heavily the stream moves ! Its load of silt is gradually settling to the bottom, yet still the water seems to drag upon the shores. Every reef of sand, every island of mud, every overhanging willow or cottonwood or handful of arrow-weed holds out a restraining hand. But slowly, patiently, winding about obstructions, cutting out new channels, creeping where it may not run, the bubbleless water works its way to the sea. The night-winds steal along its shores and pass in and out among its sedges, but there are no whispering voices; and the stars emerge and shine upon the flat floor of water, but there is no lustre. The drear desolation of it! The blare of morning sunlight does not lift the pall, nor the waving illusions of the mirage break the stillness. The Silent River moves on carrying desolation with it; and at every step the waters grow darker, darker with the stain of red—red the hue of decay.

Sluggish movement.

Stillness of river.

It was not through paucity of imagination that the old Spaniards gave the name—Colorado.* During the first fifty years after its discovery the river was christened many times, but the name that finally clung to it was the one that gave accurate and truthful description.

The river's name.

* Colorado is said to be the Spanish translation of the Piman name *buqui aquimuti*, according to the late Dr. Elliot Coues; but the Spanish word was so obviously used to denote the red color of the stream, that any translation from the Indian would seem superfluous.

You may see on the face of the globe numerous muddy Missouris, blue Rhones, and yellow Tibers ; but there is only one red river and that the Colorado. It is not exactly an earthy red, not the color of shale and clay mixed ; but the red of peroxide of iron and copper, the *sang-du-bœuf* red of oriental ceramics, the deep insistent red of things time-worn beyond memory. And *Its red color.* there is more than a veneer about the color. It has a depth that seems luminous and yet is sadly deceptive. You do not see below the surface no matter how long you gaze into it. As well try to see through a stratum of porphyry as through that water to the bottom of the river.

To call it a river of blood would be exaggeration, and yet the truth lies in the exaggeration. As one walks along its crumbling banks there is the thought of that other river that changed its hue under the outstretched rod of the prophet. *Compared with the Nile.* How weird indeed must have been the ensanguined flow of the Nile, with its little waves breaking in crests of pink foam ! How strange the shores where the receding waters left upon sand and rock a bordering line of scarlet froth ! But the Colorado is not quite like that—not so ghastly, not so unearthly. It may suggest at times the heavy welling flow of thickening blood which the sands at every step are trying to drink up; but this is suggestion only, not realization. It seems to hint at blood, and *The blood hue.* under starlight to resemble it; but the resemblance is more apparent than real. The Colorado is a red river but not a scarlet one.

It may be thought odd that the river should *River changes.* change so radically from the clear blue-green of its fountain-head to the opaque red of its desert stream, but rivers when they go wandering down to the sea usually leave their mountain purity behind them. The Colorado rushing through a thousand miles of canyons, cuts and carries seaward with it red sands of shale, *Red sands and silt.* granite, and porphyry, red rustings of iron, red grits of carnelian, agate and garnet. All the tributaries come bearing their tokens of red copper, and with the rains the whole red surface of the watershed apparently washes into the smaller creeks and thus into the valleys. When the river reaches the desert carrying its burden of silt, it no longer knows the bowlder-bed, the rocky shores, the breaking waterfalls that clarify a stream. And there are no large pools where the water can rest while the silt settles to the bottom. Besides, the desert itself at times pours into the river an even deeper red than the canyons. And it does this not through arroyos alone, but also by a wide surface drainage.

Often the slope of the desert to the river is gradual for many miles—sometimes like the top of a huge table slightly tilted from the horizontal. When the edge of the table is reached the mesa begins to break into terraces (often cut through by small gullies), and the final descent is not unlike the steps of a Roman circus leading down into the arena. During cloud-bursts the waters pour down these steps with great fury and the river simply acts as a catch-basin for all the running color of the desert.

River-banks.

The "bottom" lands, forming the immediate banks of the river, are the silt deposits of former years. Often they are several miles in width and are usually covered with arrow-weed, willows, alders, and cottonwoods. The growth is dense if not tall and often forms an almost impenetrable jungle through which are scattered little openings where grass and flowers grow and Indians build reed wickiups and raise melons and corn in season. The desert terraces on either side (sometimes there is a row of sand-dunes) come down to meet these "bottom" lands,

"Bottom" lands.

and the line where the one leaves off and the other begins is drawn as with the sharp edge of a knife.   Seen from the distant mountain tops the river moves between two long ribbons of green, and the borders are the gray and gold mesas of the desert. *The green bands.*

Afloat and drifting down between these lines of green your attention is perhaps not at first attracted by the water.   You are interested in the thickets of alders and the occasional bursts of white and yellow flowers from among the bushes.   They are very commonplace bushes, very ordinary flowers ; but how lovely they look as they seem to drift by the boat !   How silent again are these clumps of alder and willow ! There may be linnets and sparrows among them but they do not make their presence obtrusive in song.   A hawk wheels along over the arrow-weed looking for quail, but his wings cut the air without noise. How deathly still everything seems !   The water wears into the soft banks, the banks keep sloughing into the stream, but again you hear no splashing fall. *Bushes and flowers.*

And the water itself is just as soundless. There is never a sunken rock to make a little gurgle, never a strip of gravel beach where a wave could charm you with its play.   The beat *Soundless water.*

of oars breaks the air with a jar, but breaks no bubbles on the water. You look long at the stream and fall to wondering if there can be any life in it. What besides a polywog or a bullhead could live there? Obviously, and in fact—nothing. Perhaps there are otter and beaver living along the pockets in the banks? Yes; there were otter and beaver here at one time, but they are very scarce to-day. But *Wild fowl.* there are wild fowl? Yes; in the spring and fall the geese and ducks follow the river in their flights, but they do not like the red water. What proof? Because they do not stop long in any one place. They swing into a bayou or slough late at night and go out at early dawn. They do not love the stream, but wild fowl on their migratory flights must have water, and this river is the only one between the Rockies and the Pacific that runs north and south.

Herons and bitterns. The blue herons and the bitterns do not mind the red mud or the red water, in fact they rather like it; but they were always solitary people of the sedge. They prowl about the marshes alone and the swish of oars drives them into the air with a guttural "Quowk." And there are snipe here, bands of them, flashing their wings in the sun as they wheel over the red waters or trip along the muddy banks singly or in pairs. They are quite at home on the bars and bayou flats, but it seems not a very happy home for them—that is judging by the absence of snipe talk. The little teeter flies *Snipe.* ahead of you from point to point, but makes no twitter, the yellow-leg seldom sounds his mellow three-note call, and the kill-deer, even though you shoot at him, will not cry " Kill-deer ! " " Kill-deer ! "

It may be the season when birds are mute, or it may merely happen so for to-day, or it may be that the silence of the river and the desert is an oppressive influence ; but certainly you have never seen bird-life so hopelessly sad. Even *Sad bird-life.* the kingfisher, swinging down in a blue line from a dead limb and skimming the water, makes none of that rattling clatter that you knew so well when you were a child by a New England mill-stream. And what does a kingfisher on such a river as this ? If it were filled with fish he could not see them through that thick water.

The voiceless river ! From the canyon to the sea it flows through deserts, and ever the seal of silence is upon it. Even the scant life of its borders is dumb—birds with no note, animals

*The
forsaken.*

Solitude.

*Beauty of
the river.*

with no cry, human beings with no voice. And
so forsaken ! The largest river west of the
mountains and yet the least known. There are
miles upon miles of mesas stretching upward
from the stream that no feet have ever trodden,
and that possess not a vestige of life of any
kind. And along its banks the same tale is
told. You float for days and meet with no
traces of humanity. When they do appear it is
but to emphasize the solitude. An Indian
wickiup on the bank, an Indian town ; yes, a
white man's town, what impression do they
make upon the desert and its river ? You drift
by Yuma and wonder what it is doing there.
Had it been built in the middle of the Pacific
on a barren rock it could not be more isolated,
more hopelessly "at sea."

After the river crosses the border-line of
Mexico it grows broader and flatter than ever.
And still the color seems to deepen. For all its
suggestion of blood it is not an unlovely color.
On the contrary, that deep red contrasted with
the green of the banks and the blue of the sky,
makes a very beautiful color harmony. They
are hues of depth and substance—hues that
comport excellently well with the character of
the river itself. And never a river had more

character than the Colorado. You may not fancy the solitude of the stream nor its suggestive coloring, but you cannot deny its majesty and its nobility. It has not now the babble of the brook nor the swift rush of the canyon water ; rather the quiet dignity that is above conflict, beyond gayety. It has grown old, it is nearing its end ; but nothing could be calmer, simpler, more sublime, than the drift of it down into the delta basin. *Its majesty.*

The mountains are receding on every side, the desert is flattening to meet the sea, and the ocean tides are rising to meet the river. Half human in its dissolution, the river begins to break joint by joint. The change has been gradually taking place for miles and now manifests itself positively. The bottom lands widen, many channels or side-sloughs open upon the stream, and the water is distributed into the mouths of the delta. There is a break in the volume and mass—a disintegration of forces. And by divers ways, devious and slow, the crippled streams well out to the Gulf and never come together again. *The delta.* *Disintegration.*

It is not so when the river is at its height with spring freshets. Then the stream is swollen beyond its banks. All the bottom lands for miles across, up to the very terraces of the mesas, are covered ; and the red flood moves like an ocean current, vast in width, ponderous in weight, irresistible in strength. All things that can be uprooted or wrenched away, move with it. Nothing can check or stop it now. It is the Grand Canyon river once more, free, mighty, dangerous even in its death-throes.

The river during floods.

And now at the full and the change of the moon, when the Gulf waters come in like a tidal wave, and the waters of the north meet the waters of the south, there is a mighty conflict of opposing forces. The famous "bore" of the river-mouth is the result. When the forces first meet there is a slow push-up of the water which rises in the shape of a ridge or wedge. The sea-water gradually proves itself the greater and the stronger body, and the ridge breaks into a crest and pitches forward with a roar. The undercut of the river sweeps away the footing of the tide, so to speak, and flings the top of the wave violently forward. The red river rushes under, the blue tide rushes over. There is the flash and dash of parti-colored foam on the crests, the flinging of jets of spray high in air, the long roll of waves breaking not upon a beach, but upon the back of the river,

The "bore."

Meeting of river and sea.

and the shaking of the ground as though an earthquake were passing. After it is all done with and gone, with no trace of wave or foam remaining, miles away down the Gulf the red river slowly rises in little streams through the blue to the surface. There it spreads fan-like over the top of the sea, and finally mingles with and is lost in the greater body.

The river is no more. It has gone down to its blue tomb in the Gulf—the fairest tomb that ever river knew. Something of serenity in the Gulf waters, something of the monumental in the bordering mountains, something of the unknown and the undiscovered over all, make it a fit resting-place for the majestic Colorado. The lonely stream that so shunned contact with man, that dug its bed thousands of feet in the depths of pathless canyons, and trailed its length across trackless deserts, sought out instinctively a point of disappearance far from the madding crowd. The blue waters of the Gulf, the beaches of shell, the red, red mountains standing with their feet in the sea, are still far removed from civilization's touch. There are no towns or roads or people by those shores, there are no ships upon those seas, there are no dust and smoke of factories in those skies. The Indians

The blue tomb.

Shores of the Gulf.

are there as undisturbed as in the days of Coronado, and the white man is coming but has not yet arrived. The sun still shines on unknown bays and unexplored peaks. Therefore is there silence—something of the hush of the deserts and the river that flows between.

CHAPTER V

LIGHT, AIR, AND COLOR

THESE deserts, cut through from north to south by a silent river and from east to west by two noisy railways, seem remarkable for only a few commonplace things, according to the consensus of public opinion. All that one hears or reads about them is that they are very hot, that the sunlight is very glaring, and that there is a sand-storm, a thirst, and death waiting for every traveller who ventures over the first divide.

Popular ideas of the desert.

There is truth enough, to be sure, in the heat and glare part of it, and an exceptional truth in the other part of it. It is intensely hot on the desert at times, but the sun is not responsible for it precisely in the manner alleged. The heat that one feels is not direct sunlight so much as radiation from the receptive sands; and the glare is due not to preternatural brightness in the sunbeam, but to there being no reliefs for the eye in shadows, in dark colors, in

Sunlight on desert.

77

heavy foliage. The vegetation of the desert is so slight that practically the whole surface of the sand acts as a reflector ; and it is this, rather than the sun's intensity, that causes the great body of light. The white roads in Southern France, for the surface they cover, are more glaring than any desert sands ; and the sunlight upon snow in Minnesota or New England is more dazzling. In certain spots where there are salt or soda beds the combination of heat and light is bewildering enough for anyone ; but such places are rare. White is something seldom seen on desert lands, and black is an unknown quantity in my observations. Even lava, which is popularly supposed to be as black as coal, has a reddish hue about it. Everything has some color—even the air. Indeed, we shall not comprehend the desert light without a momentary study of this desert air.

Glare and heat.

The circumambient medium which we call the atmosphere is to the earth only as so much ground-glass globe to a lamp—something that breaks, checks, and diffuses the light. We have never known, never shall know, direct sunlight —that is, sunlight in its purity undisturbed by atmospheric conditions. It is a blue shaft falling perfectly straight, not a diffused white or

Pure sunlight.

yellow light ; and probably the life of the earth would not endure for an hour if submitted to its unchecked intensity. The white or yellow light, known to us as sunlight, is produced by the ground-glass globe of air, and it follows readily enough that its intensity is absolutely dependent upon the density of the atmosphere —the thickness of the globe. The cause for the thickening of the aërial envelope lies in the particles of dust, soot, smoke, salt, and vapor which are found floating in larger or smaller proportions in all atmospheres.

Atmospher- ic envelope.

In rainy countries like England and Holland the vapor particles alone are sufficiently numer- ous to cause at times great obscurity of light, as in the case of fog ; and the air is only com- paratively clear even when the skies are all blue. The light is almost always whitish, and the horizons often milky white. The air is thick, for you cannot see a mountain fifteen miles away in any sharpness of detail. There is a mistiness about the rock masses and a vague- ness about the outline. An opera-glass does not help your vision. The obscurity is not in the eyes but in the atmospheric veil through which you are striving to see. On the contrary, in the high plateau country of Wyoming, where

Vapor particles.

Clear air.

the quantities of dust and vapor in the air are comparatively small, the distances that one can see are enormous. A mountain seventy miles away often appears sharp-cut against the sky, and at sunset the lights and shadows upon its sides look only ten miles distant.

But desert air is not quite like the plateau air of Wyoming, though one can see through it for many leagues. It is not thickened by moisture particles, for its humidity is almost nothing ; but the dust particles, carried upward by radiation and the winds, answer a similar purpose. They parry the sunshaft, break and color the light, increase the density of the envelope. Dust is always present in the desert air in some degree, and when it is at its maximum with the heat and winds of July, we see the air as a blue, yellow, or pink haze. This haze is not seen so well at noonday as at evening when the sun's rays are streaming through canyons, or at dawn when it lies in the mountain shadows and reflects the blue sky. Nor does it muffle or obscure so much as the moisture-laden mists of Holland, but it thickens the air perceptibly and decreases in measure the intensity of the light.

Yet despite the fact that desert air is dustladen and must be thickened somewhat, there

Dust particles.

Hazes.

is something almost inexplicable about it. It seems so thin, so rarefied ; and it is so scentless—I had almost said breathless—that it is like no air at all. You breathe it without feeling it, you look through it without being conscious of its presence. Yet here comes in the contradiction. Desert air is very easily recognized by the eyes alone. The traveller in California when he wakes in the morning and glances out of the car-window at the air in the mountain canyons, knows instantly on which side of the Tehachepi Range the train is moving. He knows he is crossing the Mojave. The lilac-blue veiling that hangs about those mountains is as recognizable as the sea air of the Massachusetts shore. And, strange enough, the sea breezes that blow across the deserts all down the Pacific coast have no appreciable effect upon this air. The peninsula of Lower California is practically surrounded by water, but through its entire length and down the shores of Sonora to Mazatlan, there is nothing but that clear, dry air.

Seeing the desert air.

Sea breezes on desert.

I use the word " clear " because one can see so far through this atmosphere, and yet it is not clear or we should not see it so plainly. There is the contradiction again. Is it perhaps

the coloring of it that makes it so apparent ?
Probably. Even the clearest atmosphere has
some coloring about it. Usually it is an inde-
finable blue. Air-blue means the most delicate
of all colors—something not of surface depth
but of transparency, builded up by superimposed strata of air many miles perhaps in
thickness. This air-blue is seen at its best in
the gorges of the Alps, and in the mountain
distances of Scotland ; but it is not so apparent
on the desert. The coloring of the atmosphere
Different
hues. on the Colorado and the Mojave is oftener
pink, yellow, lilac, rose-color, sometimes fire-
red. And to understand that we must take up
the ground-glass globe again.

It has been said that our atmosphere breaks,
checks, and diffuses the falling sunlight like
the globe of a lamp. It does something more.
It acts as a prism and breaks the beam of sun-
Producing
color. light into the colors of the spectrum. Some of
these colors it deals with more harshly than
others because of their shortness and their
weakness. The blue rays, for instance, are the
greatest in number ; but they are the shortest
in length, the weakest in travelling power of
any of them. Because of their weakness, and
because of their affinity (as regards size) with

the small dust particles of the higher air region, great quantities of these rays are caught, refracted, and practically held in check in the *Refracted rays.* upper strata of the atmosphere. We see them massed together overhead and call them the "blue sky." After many millions of these blue rays have been eliminated from the sunlight the remaining rays come down to earth as a white or yellow or at times reddish light, dependent upon the density of the lower atmosphere.

Now it seems that an atmosphere laden with moisture particles obstructs the passage earthward of the blue rays, less perhaps than an atmosphere laden with dust. In consequence, when they are thus allowed to come down into the lower atmosphere in company with the other rays, their vast number serves to dominate the others, and to produce a cool tone of *Cold colors, how produced.* color over all. So it is that in moist countries like Scotland you will find the sky cold-blue and the air tinged gray, pale-blue, or at twilight in the mountain valleys, a chilly purple. A dust-laden atmosphere seems to act just the reverse of this. It obstructs all the rays in proportion to its density, but it stops the blue rays first, holds them in the upper air, while the stronger rays of red and yellow are only checked in the lower and thicker air-strata near the earth. The result of this is to produce a warm tone of color over all. So it is that in dry countries like Spain and Morocco or on the deserts of Africa and America, you will find the sky rose-hued or yellow, and the air lilac, pink, red, or yellow.

Warm colors.

I mean now that the air itself is colored. Of course countless quantities of light-beams and dispersed rays break through the aërial envelope and reach the earth, else we should not see color in the trees or grasses or flowers about us ; but I am not now speaking of the color of objects on the earth, but of the color of the air. A thing too intangible for color you think ? But what of the sky overhead ? It is only tinted atmosphere. And what of the bright-hued horizon skies at sunrise and sunset, the rosy-yellow skies of Indian summer ! They are only tinted atmospheres again. Banked up in great masses, and seen at long distances, the air-color becomes palpably apparent. Why then should it not be present in shorter distances, in mountain canyons, across mesas and lomas, and over the stretches of the desert plains ?

Sky colors.

The truth is all air is colored, and that of

the desert is deeper dyed and warmer hued than any other for the reasons just given. It takes on many tints at different times, dependent upon the thickening of the envelope by heat and dust-diffusing winds. I do not know if it is possible for fine dust to radiate with heat alone ; but certain it is that, without the aid of the wind, there is more dust in the air on hot days than at any other time. When the thermometer rises above 100° F., the atmosphere is heavy with it, and the lower strata are dancing and trembling with phantoms of the mirage at every point of the compass. It would seem as though the rising heat took up with it countless small dust-particles and that these were responsible for the rosy or golden quality of the air-coloring. *Color produced by dust.*

Effect of heat.

There is a more positive tinting of the air produced sometimes by high winds. The lighter particles of sand are always being drifted here and there through the aërial regions, and even on still days the whirlwinds are eddying and circling, lifting long columns of dust skyward and then allowing the dust to settle back to earth through the atmosphere. The stronger the wind, and the more of dust and sand, the brighter the coloring. The climax is reached *Effect of winds.*

in the dramatic sand-storm—a veritable sand-fog which often turns half the heavens into a luminous red, and makes the sun look like a round ball of fire.

The dust-particle in itself is sufficient to account for the warmth of coloring in the desert air—sufficient in itself to produce the pink, yellow, and lilac hazes. And yet I am tempted to suggest some other causes. It is not easy to
prove that a reflection may be thrown upward upon the air by the yellow face of the desert beneath it—a reflection similar to that produced by a fire upon a night sky—yet I believe there is something of the desert's air-coloring derived from that source. Nor is it easy to prove that a reflection is cast by blue, pink, and yellow skies, upon the lower air-strata, yet certain effects shown in the mirage (the water illusion, for instance, which seems only the reflection of the sky from heated air) seem to suggest it. And if we put together other casual observations they will make argument toward the same goal. For instance, the common blue haze that we may see any day in the mountains, is always deepest in the early morning when the blue sky over it is deepest. At noon when the sky turns gray-blue the haze turns

gray-blue also. The yellow haze of the desert is seen at its best when there is a yellow sunset, and the pink haze when there is a red sunset, indicating that at least the sky has some part in coloring by reflection the lower layers of desert air.

Blue, yellow, and pink hazes.

Whatever the cause, there can be no doubt about the effect. The desert air is practically colored air. Several times from high mountains I have seen it lying below me like an enormous tinted cloud or veil. A similar veiling of pink, lilac, or pale yellow is to be seen in the gorges of the Grand Canyon; it stretches across the Providence Mountains at noonday and is to be seen about the peaks and packed in the valleys at sunset; it is dense down in the Coahuila Basin; it is denser from range to range across the hollow of Death Valley; and it tinges the whole face of the Painted Desert in Arizona. In its milder manifestations it is always present, and during the summer months its appearance is often startling. By that I do not mean that one looks through it as through a highly colored glass. The impression should not be gained that this air is so rose-colored or saffron-hued that one has to rub his eyes and wonder if he is awake. The average unobservant traveller looks

The dust-veil.

Summer coloring.

through it and thinks it not different from
any other air. But it is different. In itself,
and in its effect upon the landscape, it is perhaps responsible for the greater part of what
everyone calls "the wonderful color" of the
desert.

Local hues.   And this not to the obliteration of local hue
in sands, rocks, and plants. Quite independent
of atmospheres, the porphyry mountains are
dull red, the grease wood is dull green, the vast
stretches of sand are dull yellow. And these
large bodies of local color have their influence in
the total sum-up. Slight as is the vegetation
upon the desert, it is surprising how it seems
to bunch together and count as a color-mass.
Almost all the growths are "evergreen." The
shrubs and the trees shed their leaves, to be sure,
but they do it so slowly that the new ones are
on before the old ones are off. The general
Greens of   appearance is always green, but not a bright
desert
plants.   hue, except after prolonged rains. Usually it
is an olive, bordering upon yellow. One can
hardly estimate what a relieving note this thin
thatch of color is, or how monotonous the
desert might be without it. It is welcome, for
it belongs to the scene, and fits in the color-
scheme of the landscape as perfectly as the

dark-green pines in the mountain scenery of Norway.

The sands, again, form vast fields of local color, and, indeed, the beds of sand and gravel, the dunes, the ridges, and the mesas, make up the most widespread local hue on the desert. The sands are not "golden," except under peculiar circumstances, such as when they are whirled high in the air by the winds, and then struck broadside by the sunlight. Lying quietly upon the earth they are usually a dull yellow. In the morning light they are often gray, at noon frequently a bleached yellow, and at sunset occasionally pink or saffron-hued. Wavering heat and mirage give them temporary coloring at times that is beautifully unreal. They then appear to undulate slightly like the smooth surface of a summer sea at sunset; and the colors shift and travel with the undulations. The appearance is not common; perfect calm, a flat plain, and intense heat being apparently the conditions necessary to its existence.

Color of sands.

Sands in mirage.

The rocks of the upper peaks and those that make the upright walls of mountains, though small in body of color, are perhaps more varied in hue than either the sands or the vegetation, and that, too, without primary notes as in the

Grand Canyon of the Yellowstone. The reds are
always salmon-colored, terra-cotta, or Indian
red; the greens are olive-hued, plum-colored,
sage-green; the yellows are as pallid as the
leaves of yellow roses. Fresh breaks in the
wall of rock may show brighter colors that
have not yet been weather-worn, or they may
reveal the oxidation of various minerals. Often
long strata and beds, and even whole mountain
tops show blue and green with copper, or
orange with iron, or purple with slates, or white
with quartz. But the tones soon become subdued. A mountain wall may be dark red with-

in, but it is weather-stained and lichen-covered
without; long-reaching shafts of granite that
loom upward from a peak may be yellow at
heart but they are silver-gray on the surface.
The colors have undergone years of " toning
down " until they blend and run together like
the faded tints of an Eastern rug.

But granted the quantity and the quality of
local colors in the desert, and the fact still re-

mains that the air is the medium that influ-
ences if it does not radically change them all.
The local hue of a sierra may be gray, dark red,
iron-hued, or lead-colored ; but at a distance,
seen through dust-laden air, it may appear

topaz-yellow, sapphire-blue, bright lilac, rose-red—yes, fire-red. During the heated months of summer such colors are not exceptional. They appear almost every evening. I have seen at sunset, looking north from Sonora some twenty miles, the whole tower-like shaft of Baboqui-vari change from blue to topaz and from topaz to glowing red in the course of half an hour. I do not mean edgings or rims or spots of these colors upon the peak, but the whole upper half of the mountain completely changed by them. The red color gave the peak the appearance of hot iron, and when it finally died out the dark dull hue that came after was like that of a clouded garnet.

Peak of Baboqui-vari.

The high ranges along the western side of Arizona, and the buttes and tall spires in the Upper Basin region, all show these warm fire-colors under heat and sunset light, and often in the full of noon. The colored air in conjunction with light is always responsible for the hues. Even when you are close up to the mountains you can see the effect of the air in small ways. There are edgings of bright color to the hill-ridges and the peaks ; and in the canyons, where perhaps a sunshaft streams across the shadow, you can see the gold or fire-color of the

Buttes and spires.

air most distinctly. Very beautiful are these golden sunshafts shot through the canyons. And the red shafts are often startling. It would seem as though the canyons were packed thick with yellow or red haze. And so in reality they are.

Sunshafts through canyons.

There is one marked departure from the uniform warm colors of the desert that should be mentioned just here. It is the clear blue seen in the shadows of western-lying mountains at sunset. This colored shadow shows only when there is a yellow or orange hued sunset, and it is produced by the yellow of the sky casting its complementary hue (blue) in the shadow. At sea a ship crossing a yellow sunset will show a marvellous blue in her sails just as she crosses the line of the sun, and the desert mountains repeat the same complementary color with equal facility and greater variety. It is not of long duration. It changes as the sky changes, but maintains always the complementary hue.

Complementary hues in shadow.

The presence of the complementary color in the shadow is exceptional, however. The shadows cast by such objects as the sahuaro and the palo verde are apparently quite colorless; and so, too, are the shadows of passing clouds. The colored shadow is produced by reflection from

Colored shadows,

the sky, mixed with something of local color in the background, and also complementary color. It is usually blue or lilac-blue, on snow for example, when there is a blue sky overhead ; and lilac when shown upon sand or a blue stone road. Perhaps it does not appear often on the Mojave-Colorado because the surfaces are too rough and broken with coarse gravel to make good reflectors of the sky. The fault is not in the light or in the sky, for upon the fine sands of the dunes, and upon beds of fine gypsum and salt, you can see your own shadow colored an absolute indigo ; and often upon bowlders of *Blue shadows upon salt-beds.* white quartz the shadows of cholla and grease wood are cast in almost cobalt hues.

All color—local, reflected, translucent, complementary—is, of course, made possible by light and has no existence apart from it. Through the long desert day the sunbeams are *How light makes color.* weaving skeins of color across the sands, along the sides of the canyons, and about the tops of the mountains. They stain the ledges of copper with turquoise, they burn the buttes to a terra-cotta red, they paint the sands with rose and violet, and they key the air to the hue of the opal. The reek of color that splashes the western sky at sunset is but the climax of the

*Desert
sunsets.*

sun's endeavor. If there are clouds stretched across the west the ending is usually one of exceptional brilliancy. The reds are all scarlet, the yellows are like burnished brass, the oranges like shining gold.

But the sky and clouds of the desert are of such unique splendor that they call for a chapter of their own.

CHAPTER VI

DESERT SKY AND CLOUDS

How silently, even swiftly, the days glide by
out in the desert, in the waste, in the wilderness! How "the morning and the evening
make up the day" and the purple shadow slips
in between with a midnight all stars! And
how day by day the interest grows in the long
overlooked commonplace things of nature! In *Common-*
place things
a few weeks we are studying bushes, bowlders, *of nature.*
stones, sand-drifts—things we never thought of
looking at in any other country. And after a
time we begin to make mental notes on the
changes of light, air, clouds, and blue sky. At
first we are perhaps bothered about the intensity of the sky, for we have always heard of the
"deep blue" that overhangs the desert; and
we expect to see it at any and all times. But
we discover that it shows itself in its greatest
depth only in the morning before sunrise. Then
it is a dark blue, bordering upon purple; and
for some time after the sun comes up it holds a

The blue sky. deep blue tinge. At noon it has passed through a whole gamut of tones and is pale blue, yellowish, lilac-toned, or rosy ; in the late afternoon it has changed again to pink or gold or orange ; and after twilight and under the moon, warm purples stretch across the whole reach of the firmament from horizon to horizon.

But the changes in the blue during the day have no constancy to a change. There is no fixed purpose about them. The caprices of light, heat, and dust control the appearances. *Changes in the blue.* Sometimes the sky at dawn is as pallid as a snow-drop with pearly grays just emerging from the blue ; and again it may be flushed with saffron, rose, and pink. When there are clouds and great heat the effect is often very brilliant. The colors are intense in chrome-yellows, golds, carmines, magentas, malachite-greens—a body of gorgeous hues upheld by enormous side wings of paler tints that encircle the horizon to the north and south, and send waves of color far up *Dawns on the desert.* the sky to the cool zenith. Such dawns are seldom seen in moist countries, nor are they usual on the desert, except during the hot summer months.

The prevailing note of the sky, the one oftenest seen, is, of course, blue—a color we may not perhaps linger over because it is so common. And yet how seldom it is appreciated! Our attention is called to it in art—in a hawthorn jar as large as a sugar-bowl, made in a certain period, in a certain Oriental school. The æsthetic world is perhaps set agog by this ceramic blue. But what are its depth and purity compared to the ethereal blue! Yet the color is beautiful in the jar and infinitely more beautiful in the sky—that is beautiful in itself and merely as color. It is not necessary that it should mean anything. Line and tint do not always require significance to be beautiful. There is no tale or text or testimony to be tortured out of the blue sky. It is a splendid body of color; no more. *Blue as a color.*

You cannot always see the wonderful quality of this sky-blue from the desert valley, because it is disturbed by reflections, by sand-storms, by lower air strata. The report it makes of itself when you begin to gain altitude on a mountain's side is quite different. At four thousand feet the blue is certainly more positive, more intense, than at sea-level; at six thousand feet it begins to darken and deepen, and it seems to fit in the saddles and notches of the mountains like a block of lapis lazuli; at eight thousand feet it *Sky from mountain heights.*

The night sky.

has darkened still more and has a violet hue about it. The night sky at this altitude is almost weird in its purples. A deep violet fits up close to the rim of the moon, and the orb itself looks like a silver wafer pasted upon the sky.

The darkening of the sky continues as the height increases. If one could rise to, say, fifty thousand feet, he would probably see the sun only as a shining point of light, and the firmament merely as a blue-black background. The diffusion of light must decrease with the growing thinness of the atmospheric envelope. At what point it would cease and the sky become perfectly black would be difficult to say, but certainly the limit would be reached when our atmosphere practically ceased to exist. Space

Blackness of space.

from necessity must be black except where the straight beams of light stream from the sun and the stars.

Bright sky-colors.

The bright sky-colors, the spectacular effects, are not to be found high up in the blue of the dome. The air in the zenith is too thin, too free from dust, to take deep colorings of red and orange. Those colors belong near the earth, along the horizons where the aërial envelope is dense. The lower strata of atmosphere are in fact responsible for the gorgeous sunsets, the tinted hazes, the Indian-summer skies, the hot September glows. These all appear in their splendor when the sun is near the horizon-line *Horizon skies.* and its beams are falling through the many miles of hot, dust-laden air that lie along the surface of the earth. The air at sunset after a day of intense heat-radiation is usually so thick that only the long and strong waves of color can pass through it. The blues are almost lost, the neutral tints are missing, the greens are seen but faintly. The waves of red and yellow are the only ones that travel through the thick air with force. And these are the colors that tell us the story of the desert sunset.

Ordinarily the sky at evening over the desert, when seen without clouds, shows the colors of *Spectrum colors.* the spectrum beginning with red at the bottom and running through the yellows, greens, and blues up to the purple of the zenith. In cool weather, however, this spectrum arrangement seems swept out of existence by a broad band of yellow-green that stretches half way *Bands of yellow.* around the circle. It is a pale yellow fading into a pale green, which in turn melts into a pale blue. In hot weather this pallor is changed to something much richer and deeper. A band of orange takes its place. It is a flame-colored orange, and its hue is felt in reflection upon valley, plain, and mountain peak. This indeed is the orange light that converts the air in the mountain canyons into golden mist, and is measurably responsible for the yellow sunshafts that, streaming through the pinnacles of the western mountains, reach far across the upper sky in ever-widening bands. This great orange belt is lacking in that variety and vividness of coloring that comes with clouds, but it is not wanting in a splendor of its own. It is the broadest, the simplest, and in many respects the sublimest sunset imaginable—a golden dream with the sky enthroned in glory and the earth at its feet reflecting its lustre.

The orange sky.

But the more brilliant sunsets are only seen when there are broken translucent clouds in the west. There are cloudy days even on the desert. After many nights of heat, long skeins of white stratus will gather along the horizons, and out of them will slowly be woven forms of the cumulus and the nimbus. And it will rain in short squalls of great violence on the lomas, mesas, and bordering mountains. But usually the cloud that drenches a mountain top eight thousand feet up will pass over an

Desert clouds.

intervening valley, pouring down the same flood of rain, and yet not a drop of it reaching the ground. The air is always dry and the rain-drop that has to fall through eight thousand feet of it before reaching the earth, never gets there. It is evaporated and carried up to its parent cloud again. During the so-called "rainy season" you may frequently see clouds all about the horizon and overhead that are "raining" —letting down long tails and sheets of rain that are plainly visible; but they never touch the earth. The sheet lightens, breaks, and dissipates two thousand feet up. It rains, true enough, but there is no water, just as there are desert rivers, but they have no visible stream. That is the desert of it both above and below.

Rainfall.

With the rain come trooping almost all the cloud-forms known to the sky. And the thick ones like the nimbus carry with them a chilling, deadening effect. The rolls and sheets of rain-clouds that cover the heavens at times rob the desert of light, air, and color at one fell swoop. Its beauty vanishes as by magic. Instead of colored haze there is gray gloom settling along the hills and about the mesas. The sands lose their lustre and become dull and formless, the vegetation darkens to a dead gray, and the

Effect of the nimbus.

mountains turn slate-colored, mouldy, unwholesome looking. A mantle of drab envelops the scene, and the glory of the desert has departed.

All the other cloud-forms, being more or less transparent, seem to aid rather than to obscure the splendor of the sky. The most common clouds of all are the cumuli. In hot summer afternoons they gather and heap up in huge masses with turrets and domes of light that reach at times forty thousand feet above the earth. At sunset they begin to show color before any of the other clouds. If seen against the sun their edges at first gleam silver-white and then change to gold; if along the horizon to the north or south, or lying back in the eastern sky, they show dazzling white like a snowy Alp. As the sun disappears below the line they begin to warm in color, turning yellow, pink, and rose. Finally they darken into lilac and purple, then sink and disappear entirely. The smaller forms of cumulus that appear in the west at evening are always splashes of sunset color, sometimes being shot through with yellow or scarlet. They ultimately appear floating against the night sky as spots of purple and gray.

Above the cumuli and often flung across them like bands of gauze, are the strati—clouds of

Cumuli.

Heap clouds at sunset.

Strati.

the middle air region. This veil or sheet-cloud might be called a twilight cloud, giving out as it does its greatest splendor after the sun has disappeared below the verge. It then takes all colors and with singular vividness. At times it will overspread the whole west as a sheet of brilliant magenta, but more frequently it blares with scarlet, carmine, crimson, flushing up and then fading out, shifting from one color to another; and finally dying out in a beautiful ashes of roses. When these clouds and all their variations have faded into lilac and deep purples, there are still bright spots of color in the upper sky where the cirri are receiving the last rays of the sun.

The cirrus with its many feathery and fleecy *Cirri.* forms is the thinnest, the highest, and the most brilliant in light of all the clouds. Perhaps its brilliancy is due to its being an ice-cloud. It seems odd that here in the desert with so much heat rising and tempering the upper air there should be clouds of ice but a few miles above it. *Ice-clouds.* The cirrus and also the higher forms of the cumulo-stratus are masses of hoar-frost, spicules of ice floating in the air, instead of tiny globules of vapor.

There is nothing remarkable about the desert

clouds—that is nothing very different from the clouds of other countries—except in light, color, and background. They appear incomparably *Clouds of fire.* more brilliant and fiery here than elsewhere on the globe. The colors, like everything else on the desert, are intense in their power, fierce in their glare. They vibrate, they scintillate, they penetrate and tinge everything with their hue. And then, as though heaping splendor upon splendor, what a wonderful background they are woven upon ! Great bands of orange, green, and blue that all the melted and fused gems in the world could not match for translucent *The celestial tapestry.* beauty. Taken as a whole, as a celestial tapestry, as a curtain of flame drawn between night and day, and what land or sky can rival it !

After the clouds have all shifted into purples and the western sky has sunk into night, then up from the east the moon — the misshapen *The desert moon.* orange-hued desert moon. How large it looks ! And how it warms the sky, and silvers the edges of the mountain peaks, and spreads its wide light across the sands ! Up, up it rises, losing something of its orange and gaining something in symmetry. In a few hours it is high in the heavens and has a great aureole of color about it. Look at the ring for a moment and you will see all the spectrum colors arranged in order. Pale hues they are but they are all there. Rainbows by day and rainbows by night! Radiant circles of colored light—not one but many. Arches above arches—not two or three but five solar bows in the sky at one time! What strange tales come out of the wilderness! But how much stranger, how much more weird and extraordinary the things that actually happen in this desert land.

Rings and rainbows.

High in the zenith rides the desert moon. What a flood of light comes from it! What pale, phosphorescent light! Under it miles and miles of cactus and grease wood are half revealed, half hidden; and far away against the dark mountains the dunes of the desert shine white as snow-clad hills in December. The stars are forth, the constellations in their places, the planets large and luminous, yet none of them has much color or sparkle. The moon dims them somewhat, but even without the moon they have not the twinkle of the stars in higher, colder latitudes. The desert air seems to veil their lustre somewhat, and yet as points of light set in that purple dome of sky how beautiful they are!

Moonlight.

Stars.

Lying down there in the sands of the desert,

The mid-
night sky.

alone and at night, with a saddle for your pil-
low, and your eyes staring upward at the stars,
how incomprehensible it all seems! The immensity and the mystery are appalling; and
yet how these very features attract the thought
and draw the curiosity of man. In the presence of the unattainable and the insurmountable we keep sending a hope, a doubt, a query,
up through the realms of air to Saturn's
throne. What key have we wherewith to un-
lock that door? We cannot comprehend a tiny
flame of our own invention called electricity,
yet we grope at the meaning of the blazing
splendor of Arcturus. Around us stretches

Alone in the
desert.

the great sand-wrapped desert whose mystery
no man knows, and not even the Sphinx could
reveal; yet beyond it, above it, upward still
upward, we seek the mysteries of Orion and
the Pleiades.

The
mysteries.

What is it that draws us to the boundless and
the fathomless? Why should the lovely things
of earth—the grasses, the trees, the lakes, the
little hills — appear trivial and insignificant
when we come face to face with the sea or the
desert or the vastness of the midnight sky? Is
it that the one is the tale of things known and
the other merely a hint, a suggestion of the un-

known? Or have immensity, space, magnitude *Space and immensity.* a peculiar beauty of their own? Is it not true that bulk and breadth are primary and essential qualities of the sublime in landscape? And is it not the sublime that we feel in immensity and mystery? If so, perhaps we have a partial explanation of our love for sky and sea and desert waste. They are the great elements. We do not see, we hardly know if their boundaries are limited; we only feel their immensity, their mystery, and their beauty.

And quite as impressive as the mysteries are the silences. Was there ever such a stillness as *The silences.* that which rests upon the desert at night! Was there ever such a hush as that which steals from star to star across the firmament! You perhaps think to break the spell by raising your voice in a cry; but you will not do so again. The sound goes but a little way and then seems to come back to your ear with a suggestion of insanity about it.

A cry in the night! Overhead the planets in their courses make no sound, the earth is still, the very animals are mute. Why then the cry of the human? How it jars the harmo- *The cry of the human.* nies! How it breaks in discord upon the unities of earth and air and sky! Century after century that cry has gone up, mobbing high heaven ; and always insanity in the cry, insanity in the crier. What folly to protest where none shall hear ! There is no appeal from the law of nature. It was made for beast and bird and creeping thing. Will the human never learn that in the eye of the law he is not different from the things that creep ?

CHAPTER VII

ILLUSIONS

In our studies of landscape we are very frequently made the victims of either illusion or delusion. The eye or the mind deceives us, and sometimes the two may join forces to our complete confusion. We are not willing to admit different reports of an appearance. The Anglo - Saxon in us insists that there can be only one truth, and everything else must be error. It is known, for instance, that Castle Dome, which looks down on the Colorado River from Western Arizona, is a turret of granite— gray, red, brown, rock-colored, whatever color you please. With that antecedent knowledge in mind how difficult it is for us to believe the report of our eyes which says that at sunset the dome is amethystine, golden, crimson, or perhaps lively purple. The reality is one thing, the appearance quite another thing ; but why are not both of them truthful ?

Reality and appearance.

And how very shy people are about accepting

a pink air, a blue shadow, or a field of yellow grass—sunlit lemon-yellow grass ! They have been brought up from youth to believe that air is colorless, that shadows are brown or gray or sooty black, and that grass is green—bottle-green. The preconceived impression of the mind refuses to make room for the actual impression of the eyes, and in consequence we are misled and deluded.

Preconceived impressions.

But do the eyes themselves always report the truth ? Yes ; the truth of appearances, but as regards the reality they may deceive you quite as completely as the mind deceives you about the apparent. And for the deception of the eyes there is no wizard's cell or magician's cabinet so admirably fitted for jugglery as this bare desert under sunlight. Its combination of light and air seem like reflecting mirrors that forever throw the misshapen image in unexpected places, in unexpected lights and colors.

Deception by sunlight.

Distorted forms and colors.

What, for instance, could be more perplexing than the odd distortions in the forms and colors of the desert mountains ! A range of these mountains may often look abnormally grand, even majestic in the early morning as they stand against the eastern sky. The outlines of the ridges and peaks may be clear cut, the light

and shade of the canyons and barrancas well
marked, the cool morning colors of the face-
walls and foot-hills distinctly placed and holding their proper value in the scene.   But by
noon the whole range has apparently lost its
lines and shrunken in size.   Under the beating
rays of the sun and surrounded by wavering
heated atmosphere its shadow masses have been
grayed down, neutralized, perhaps totally oblit-
erated ; and the long mountain surface appears *Changed appearance of moun-tains.*
as flat as a garden wall, as smooth as a row of
sand-dunes.   There is no indication of barranca or canyon.   The air has a blue-steel glow
that muffles light and completely wrecks color.
Seen through it the escarpments show only
dull blue and gray.   All the reds, yellows, and
pinks of the rocks are gone ; the surfaces wear
a burnt-out aspect as though fire had eaten into
them and left behind only a comb of volcanic
ash.

At evening, however, the range seems to return to its majesty and magnitude.   The peaks
reach up, the bases broaden, the walls break
into gashes, the ridges harden into profiles.
The sun is westering, and the light falling *Changes in line, light, and color.*
more obliquely seems to bring out the shadows
in the canyons and barrancas.   Last of all the

colors come slowly back to their normal condition, as the flush of life to one recovering
from a trance. One by one they begin to glow
on chasm, wall, and needled summit. The air,
too, changes from steel-blue to yellow, from yellow to pink, from pink to lilac, until at last
with the sun on the rim of the earth, the mountains, the air, the clouds, and the sky are all
glowing with the tints of ruby, topaz, rose-dia-
mond—hues of splendor, of grandeur, of glory.

Suppose, if you please, a similar range of
mountains thirty miles away on the desert.
Even at long distance it shows an imposing
bulk against the sky, and you think if you were
close to it, wall and peak would loom colossal.
How surprised you are then as you ride toward
it, hour after hour, to find that it does not seem
to grow in size. When you reach the foot-hills
the high mountains seem little larger than when
seen at a distance. You are further surprised
that what appeared like a flat-faced range with
its bases touching an imaginary curb-stone for
miles, is in reality a group-range with retiring
mountains on either side that lead off on acute
angles. The group is round, and has as much
breadth as length. And still greater is your
surprise when you discover that the green top

of the gray-based mountain, which has been puzzling you for so many hours, does not belong to the gray base at all. It is a pine-clad top resting upon another and more massive base far back in the group. It is the highest and most central peak of the range.

Such illusions are common, easily explained ; and yet, after all, not so easily understood. They are caused by false perspective, which in turn is caused by light and air. On the desert, perspective is always erratic. Bodies fail to detach themselves one from another, foreshortening is abnormal, the planes of landscape are flattened out of shape or telescoped, objects are huddled together or superimposed one upon another. The disturbance in aërial perspective is just as bad. Colors, lights, and shadows fall into contradictions and denials, they shirk and bear false witness, and confuse the judgment of the most experienced.

False perspective.

Abnormal foreshortening.

Contradictions and denials.

No wonder amid this distortion of the natural, this wreck of perspective, that distance is such a proverbially unknown quantity. It is the one thing the desert dweller speaks about with caution. It may be thirty or fifty miles to that picacho—he is afraid to hazard a guess. If you should go up to the top of your mountain range

Deceptive distances.

and look at the valley beyond it, the distance across might seem very slight. You can easily see to where another mountain range begins and trails away into the distance. Perhaps you fancy a few hours' ride will take you over that valley-plain to where the distant foot-hills are lying soft and warm at the bases of the mountains. You may be right and then again you may be wrong. You may spend two days getting to those foot-hills.

This deception of distance is not infrequently accompanied by fatal consequences. The inexperienced traveller thinks the distance short, he can easily get over the ground in a few hours. But how the long leagues drag out, spin out, reach out! The day is gone and he is not there, the slight supply of water is gone and he is not there, his horse is gone and he himself is going, but he is not there. The story and its ending are familiar to those who live near the desert, for every year some mining or exploring party is lost. If there are any survivors they usually make the one report: "The distance seemed so short." But there are no short distances on the desert. Every valley-plain is an immense wilderness of space.

There is another illusion—a harmless one—

Dangers of the desert.

Immensity of valley- plains.

that has not to do with perspective but with shadow and local color. The appearance is that of shadows cast down along the mountain's side by the ridges or hogbacks. Any little patch of shadow is welcome on the desert, particularly upon the mountains which are always so strongly flooded with light. But this is only a counterfeit presentment. The ridges have no vegetation upon them to hold in place the soil and rocks and these are continually breaking away into land-slips. The slips or slides expose to view streaks of local color such as may be seen in veins of iron and copper, in beds of lignite or layers of slate. It is these streaks and patches of dark color that have broken away and slipped down the mountain side under the ridges that give the appearance of shadows. They have the true value in light, and are fair to look upon even though they are deception. The weather-beaten rocks of a talus under a peak may create a similar illusion, but the shadow effect loses a velvety quality which it has when seen under the ridges.

Shadow illusions.

Color-patches on mountains.

The illusion of a cloud-shadow resting upon the foot-hills or in the valley, is frequently produced by the local color of lava-beds. Lava may be of almost any color, but when seen close to view it is usually a reddish-black. At a distance, however, and as a mass, its beds have the *Illusion of lava-beds.* exact value of a cloud-shadow. Any eye would be deceived by it. The great inundations of lava that have overrun the plains and oozed down the foot-hills and around the lomas (particularly on the Mojave) look the shadow to the very life. The beds are usually hedged about on all sides by banks of fine sand that seem to *Appearance of cloud-shadows.* stand for sunlight surrounding the shadow, and thus the deception is materially augmented. Many times I have looked up at the sky to be sure there was no cloud there, so palpable is this lava shadow-illusion.

But perhaps the most beautiful deception known to the desert is the one oftenest seen *Mirage.* —mirage. Everyone is more or less familiar with it, for it appears in some form wherever the air is heated, thickened, or has strata of different densities. It shows on the water, on the grass plains, over ploughed fields or gravel roads, on roadbeds of railways ; but the bare desert with its strong heat-radiation is primarily its home. The cause of its appearance —or at least one of its appearances—is familiar knowledge, but it may be well to state it in *Definition.* dictionary terms : " An optical illusion due to excessive bending of light-rays in traversing adjacent layers of air of widely different densities, whereby distorted, displaced, or inverted images are produced." *

This is no doubt the true explanation of that form of mirage in which people on Sahara see caravans in the sky trailing along, upside down, like flies upon the ceiling ; or on the ocean see ships hanging in the air, masts and sails downward. But the explanation is very general and is itself in some need of explanation. Perhaps then I may be pardoned for trying to illustrate the theory of mirage in my own way.

Need of explanation.

The rays of light that come from the sun to the earth appear to travel in a straight line, but they never do. As soon as they meet with and pass into the atmospheric envelope they are bent or deflected from their original direction and reach the earth by obtuse angles or in long descending curves like a spent rifle ball. This bending of the rays is called refraction, which must not be confounded with reflection—a something quite different. Now refraction is, of course, the greatest where the atmosphere is the densest. The thicker the air the more acute the bending of the light-ray. Hence the thick lay-

Refraction of light-rays.

* Century Dictionary.

ers of air lying along or a few feet above the surface of the earth on a hot day are peculiarly well-fitted to distort the light-ray, and consequently well-fitted to produce the effect of mir- *Dense air-strata.* age. These layers of air are of varying densities. Some are thicker than others ; and in this respect the atmosphere bears a resemblance to an ordinary photographic or telescopic lens. Let us use the lens illustration for a moment and perhaps it will aid comprehension of the subject.

Illustration of camera lens. You know that the lens, like the air, is of varying thicknesses or densities, and you know that in the ordinary camera the rays of light, passing through the upper part of the lens, are refracted or bent toward the perpendicular so that they reach the ground-glass " finder " at the bottom ; and that the rays passing through the lower part of the lens go to the top of the " finder." The result is that you have on the " finder " or the negative something reversed—things upside down. That, so far as the reversed image goes, is precisely the case in mirage. The air-layers act as a lens and bend the light-rays so that when seen in our " finder " —the eye—the bottom of a tree, for example, goes to the top and the top goes to the bottom.

But there is something more to mirage than this reversed image. The eyes do not see things "in their place," but see them hanging in the air as in the case of ships and caravans. To explain this, in the absence of a diagram, we shall have to take up another illustration. Suppose a light-ray so violently bent by the heat *The bent light-ray.* lying above a sidewalk that it should come to us around a street corner, and thereby we should see a man coming up a side street that lies at right angles to us. He would appear to our eyes to be coming up, not the side street, but the street we are standing in. The man, to all appearances, would not be "in his place." We should see him where he is not.

Now suppose again instead of the light-rays bending to right or left (as in the street-corner illustration), we consider them as bending skyward or earthward. Suppose yourself at sea and that you are looking up into the sky above the horizon. You see there a ship "out of its *Ships at sea.* place," hanging in the air in an impossible manner—something which is equivalent, or at least analogous, to looking down the street and seeing the image of the man around the corner. You are looking straight into the sky, yet seeing a ship below the verge. The light-rays coming from the ship on the water describe an obtuse angle or curve in reaching the eye. The rays from the bottom of the ship, lying in a dense part of the air-lens, are more acutely bent than those from the masts, and hence they go to the top of the photographic plate or your field of vision, whereas the rays from the ship's masts, being in a thinner atmosphere, are less violently bent, and thus go to the bottom of your field of vision. The result is the ship high in air above the horizon-line and upside down.

Ships up-side down.

The illusion or deception consists in this: We usually see things in flat trajectory, so to speak. Light comes to us in comparatively straight rays. The mind, therefore, has formulated a law that we see only by straight rays. In the case of mirage the light comes to us on curved, bent, or angular rays. The eyes recognize this, but the mind refuses to believe it and hence is deceived. We think we see the ship in the air by the straight ray, but in reality we see the ship *on the water* by the bent ray. It is thus that ships are often seen when far below the horizon-line, and that islands in the sea below the ocean's rim, and so far away as a hundred miles, are seen looming in the air. " Looming " is the word that describes the excessive

Wherein the illusion.

apparent elevation of the object in the sky and is more striking on sea than land. Captains of vessels often tell strange tales of how high in the air, ships and towns and coasts are seen. The report has even come back from Alaska of a city seen in the sky that is supposed to be the city of Bristol. In tropical countries and over warm ocean-currents there are often very acute bendings of the light-rays. Why may it not be so in colder lands with colder currents ?

"Looming" of vessels, islands, and cities.

The form of mirage that gives us the reversed image is seen on the desert as well as on the sea ; but not frequently—at least not in my experience. There is an illusion of mountains hanging peak downward from the sky, but one may wander on the deserts for months and never see it. The reality and the phantom both appear in the view—the phantom seeming to draw up and out of the original in a distorted, cloud-like shape. It is almost always misshapen, and as it rises high in air it seems to be detached from the original by currents of air drifted in between. More familiar sights are the appearances of trees, animals, houses, wagons, all hanging in the air in enlarged and elongated shapes and, of course, reversed. I have seen horses hitched to a wagon hanging

Reversed image of mountains.

Horses and cattle in mirage.

high up in the air with the legs of the horses twenty feet long and the wagon as large as a cabin. The stilted antelope "forty feet high and upside down" is as seldom seen in the sky as upon the earth; but desert cattle in bunches of half a dozen will sometimes walk about on the aërial ceiling in a very astonishing way.

Yet these, too, are infrequent appearances.

Illusion of rising buttes.

Nor is the illusion of buttes rising from the plain in front of you often seen. It happens only when there are buttes at one side or the other, and, I presume, this mirage is caused by the bending of the light-rays to the right or left. It presents certainly a very beautiful effect. The buttes rise up from the ground, first one and then another, until there is a range of them that holds the appearance of reality perhaps for hours, and then gradually fades out like a stereopticon picture—the bases going first and the tops gradually melting into the sky. When seen at sunset against a yellow sky the effect is magnificent. The buttes, even in illusion, take on a wonderful blue hue (the complementary color of yellow), and they seem to drift upon the sky as upon an open sea.

The bending of the light-rays to either side

instead of up or down, as following the perpendicular, may or may not be of frequent occurrence. I do not even know if the butte appearance is to be attributed to that. The opportunity to see it came to me but once, and I had not then the time to observe whether the buttes in the mirage had sides the reverse of the originals. Besides, it is certain that mirage is caused in other ways than by the bending of light-rays. The most common illusion of the desert is the water-mirage and that is caused by reflection, not refraction. Its usual appearance is that of a lake or sea of water with what looks at a distance to be small islands in it. There are those with somewhat more lively imagination than their fellows who can see cows drinking in the water, trees along the margin of the shore (palms usually), and occasionally a farm-house, a ship, or a whale. I have never seen any of these wonderful things, but the water and island part of the illusion is to be seen almost anywhere in the desert basins during hot weather. In the lower portions of the Colorado it sometimes spreads over thousands of acres, and appears not to move for hours at a stretch. At other times the wavering of the heat or the swaying of the air strata, or a change in the

Other causes for mirage.

Water-mirage.

The lake appearance.

density of the air will give the appearance of waves or slight undulations on the water. In *How produced.* either case the illusion is quite perfect. Water lying in such a bed would reflect the exact color of the sky over it ; and what the eyes really see in this desert picture is the reflection of the sky not from water but from strata of thick air.

This illusion of water is probably seen more perfectly in the great dry lake-beds of the desert where the ground is very flat and there is no vegetation, than elsewhere. In the old Coahuila Valley region of the Colorado the water comes up very close to you and the more you flatten the angle of reflection by flattening yourself upon the ground, the closer the water approaches. *Objects in the water.* The objects in it which people imagine look like familiar things are certainly very near. And these objects—wild-fowl, bushes, tufts of swamp grass, islands, buttes—are frequently bewildering because some of them are right side up and some of them are not. Some are reversed in the air and some are quietly resting upon the ground.

It happens at times that the whole picture is confused by the light-rays being both reflected *Confused mirage.* and refracted, and in addition that the rays from certain objects come to us in a direct line.

The ducks, reeds, and tufts of grass, for instance, are only clods of dirt or sand-banked bushes which are detached at the bottom by heavy drifts of air. We see their tops right side up by looking through the air-layer or some broken portion of it. But in the same scene there may be trees upside down, and mountains seen in reflection, drawn out to stupendous proportions. In the Salton Basin one hot day in September a startled coyote very obligingly ran through a most brilliant water-mirage lying directly before me. I could only see his head and part of his shoulders, for the rest of him was cut off by the air-layer ; but the appearance was that of a wolf swimming rapidly across a lake of water. *The swimming wolf.* The illusion of the water was exact enough because it was produced by reflection, but there was no illusion about the upper part of the coyote. The rays of light from his head and shoulders came to me unrefracted and unreflected—came as light usually travels from object to eye.

But refracted or reflected, every feature of the water-mirage is attractive. And sometimes its kaleidoscopic changes keep the fancy moving at a pretty pace. The appearance and disappearance of the objects and colors in the mirage

Colors and shadows in mirage.

are often quite wonderful. The reversed mountain peaks, with light and shade and color upon them, wave in and out of the imaginary lake, and are perhaps succeeded by undulations of horizon colors in grays and pinks, by sunset skies and scarlet clouds, or possibly by the white cap of a distant sierra that has been caught in the angle of reflection.

But with all its natural look one is at loss to understand how it could ever be seriously accepted as a fact, save at the first blush. People dying for water and in delirium run toward it —at least the more than twice-told tales of travellers so report—but I never knew any healthy eye that did not grow suspicious of it after the

Trembling air.

first glance. It trembles and glows too much and soon reveals itself as something intangible, hardly of earth, little more than a shifting fantasy. You cannot see it clear-cut and well-defined, and the snap-shot of your camera does not catch it at all.

Yet its illusiveness adds to, rather than detracts from, its beauty. Rose-colored dreams are always delightful ; and the mirage is only a dream. It has no more substantial fabric than the golden haze that lies in the canyons at sunset. It is only one of nature's veilings which she puts on or off capriciously. But again its *Beauty of mirage.* loveliness is not the less when its uncertain, fleeting character is revealed. It is one of the desert's most charming features because of its strange light and its softly glowing opaline color. And there we have come back again to that beauty in landscape which lies not in the lines of mountain valley and plain, but in the almost formless masses of color and light.

CHAPTER VIII

CACTUS AND GREASE WOOD

Views of Nature.

NATURE seems a benevolent or a malevolent goddess just as our own inadequate vision happens to see her. If we have eyes only for her creative beauties we think her all goodness ; if we see only her power of destruction we incline to think she is all evil. With what infinite care and patience, worthy only of a good goddess, does she build up the child, the animal, the bird, the tree, the flower ! How wonderfully she fits each for its purpose, rounding it with strength, energy, and grace ; and beautifying it with a prodigality of colors. For twenty years she works night and day to bring the child to perfection, for twenty days she toils upon the burnished wings of some insect buzzing in the sunlight, for twenty hours she paints the gold upon the petals of the dandelion. And then what ? What of the next twenty ? Does she leave her handiwork to take care of itself until an unseen dragon called Decay comes

128

along to destroy it? Not at all. The good goddess has a hand that builds up. Yes; and she has another hand that takes down. The marvellous skill of the one has its complement, its counterpart, in the other. Block by block she takes apart the mosaic with just as much deftness as she put it together.

Growth and decay.

Those first twenty years of our life we were allowed to sap blood and strength from our surroundings; the last twenty years of our life our surroundings are allowed to sap blood and strength from us. It is Nature's plan and it is carried out without any feeling. With the same indifferent spirit that she planted in us an eye to see or an ear to hear, she afterward plants a microbe to breed and a cancer to eat. She in herself is both growth and decay. The virile and healthy things of the earth are hers; and so, too, are disease, dissolution, and death. The flower and the grass spring up, they fade, they wither; and Nature neither rejoices in the life nor sorrows in the death. She is neither good nor evil; she is only a great law of change that passeth understanding. The gorgeous pageantry of the earth with all its beauty, the life thereon with its hopes and fears and struggles, and we a part of the universal whole, are brought

Nature's plan.

The law of change. up from the dust to dance on the green in the sunlight for an hour ; and then the procession that comes after us turns the sod and we creep back to Mother Earth. All, all to dust again ; and no man to this day knoweth the why thereof.

One is continually assailed with queries of this sort whenever and wherever he begins to study Nature. He never ceases to wonder why *Nature foiling her own plans.* she should take such pains to foil her own plans and bring to naught her own creations. Why did she give the flying fish such a willowy tail and such long fins, why did she labor so industriously to give him power of flight, when at the same time she was giving another fish in the sea greater strength, and a bird in the air greater swiftness wherewith to destroy him ? Why should she make the tarantula such a powerful engine of destruction when she was in the same hour making his destroyer, the tarantula-wasp ? And always here in the desert the question comes up : Why should Nature give these shrubs and plants such powers of endurance and resistance, and then surround them by heat, *Attack and defence.* drouth, and the attacks of desert animals ? It is existence for a day, but sooner or later the growth goes down and is beaten into dust.

The individual dies. Yes ; but not the species.

Perhaps now we are coming closer to an understanding of Nature's method. It is the species
that she designs to last, for a period at least ;
and the individual is of no great importance,
merely a sustaining factor, one among millions
requiring continual renewal. It is a small mat- *Preserva-tion of the species.*
ter whether there are a thousand acres of grease
wood more or less, but it is important that the
family be not extinguished. It grows readily
in the most barren spots, is very abundant and
very hardy, and hence is protected only by an
odor and a varnish. On the contrary take the
bisnaga—a rather rare cactus. It has only a
thin, short tap-root, therefore it has an enormous upper reservoir in which to store water,
and a most formidable armor of fish-hook
shaped spines that no beast or bird can pene- *Means of preserva-tion.*
trate. Remove the danger which threatens the
extinction of the family and immediately Nature removes the defensive armor. On the
desert, for instance, the yucca has a thorn like
a point of steel. Follow it from the desert into the high tropical table-lands of Mexico where
there is plenty of soil and moisture, plenty of
chance for yuccas to thrive, and you will find
it turned into a tree, and the thorn merely a
dull blade-ending. Follow the sahuaro and the

pitahaya into the tropics again, and with their cousin, the organ cactus, you find them growing a soft thorn that would hardly penetrate clothing. Abundance of soil and rain, abundance of other vegetation for browsing animals, and there is no longer need of protection. With it the family would increase too rapidly.

So it seems that Nature desires neither increase nor decrease in the species. She wishes to maintain the *status quo*. And for the sake of keeping up the general healthfulness and virility of her species she requires that there shall be change in the component parts. Each must suffer not a "sea change," but a chemical change ; and passing into liquids, gases, or dusts, still from the grave help on the universal plan. So it is that though Nature dips each one of her desert growths into the Styx to make them invulnerable, yet ever she holds them by the heel and leaves one point open to the destroying arrow.

Maintaining the status quo.

Yet it is remarkable how Nature designs and prepares the contest — the struggle for life — that is continually going on in her world. How wonderfully she arms both offence and defence ! What grounds she chooses for the conflict ! What stern conditions she lays down ! Given a

The plant-struggle for life.

waste of sand and rock, given a heat so intense that under a summer sun the stones will blister a bare foot like hot iron, given perhaps two or three inches of rain in a twelvemonth ; and what vegetation could one expect to find growing there ? Obviously, none at all. But no ; Nature insists that something shall fight *Fighting heat and drouth.* heat and drouth even here, and so she designs strange growths that live a starved life, and bring forth after their kind with much labor. Hardiest of the hardy are these plants and just as fierce in their way as the wild-cat. You cannot touch them for the claw. They have no idea of dying without a struggle. You will find every one of them admirably fitted to endure. They are marvellous engines of resistance.

The first thing that all these plants have to fight against is heat, drouth, and the evaporation of what little moisture they may have. And here Nature has equipped them with ingenuity and cunning. Not all are designed alike, to be sure, but each after its kind is good. There are the cacti, for example, that will grow where *Prevention of evaporation.* everything else perishes. Why ? For one reason because they have geometrical forms that prevent loss from evaporation by contracting a

minimum surface for a given bulk of tissue.*
There is no waste, no unnecessary exposure of
surface. Then there are some members of the
family like the "old man" cactus, that have
thick coatings of spines and long hairy growths
that prevent the evaporation of moisture by
keeping off the wind. Then again the cacti

Absence of large leaves. have no leaves to tempt the sun. Many of the
desert growths are so constructed. Even such
a tree as the lluvia d'oro has needles rather than
leaves, though it does put forth a row of tiny
leaves near the end of the needle ; and when we
come to examine the ordinary trees such as the
mesquite, the depua, the palo breya, the palo
verde, and all the acacia family, we find they
have very narrow leaves that have a fashion of
hanging diagonally to the sun and thus avoiding the direct rays. Nature is determined that

Exhaust of moisture. there shall be no unnecessary exhaust of moisture through foliage. The large-leafed bush or
tree does not exist. The best shade to be found
on the desert is under the mesquite, and unless
it is very large, the sun falls through it easily
enough.

* I am indebted to Professor Forbes of the University
of Arizona for this and several other statements in connection with desert vegetation.

As an extra precaution some shrubs are given a shellac-like sap or gum with which they varnish their leaves and make evaporation almost impossible. The ordinary greasewood is an example of this; and perhaps because of its varnish, it is, with the cacti, the hardiest of all the desert growths. It is found wherever anything living is found, and flourishes under the fiercest heat. Its leaves always look bright and have a sticky feeling about them as though recently shellacked. *Gums and varnishes of bushes.*

There are other growths that seem to have a fine sense of discretion in the matter of danger, for they let fall all their leaves at the first approach of drouth. The ocatilla, or "candle wood" as it is sometimes called, puts out a long row of bright leaves along its stems after a rain, but as soon as drouth comes it sheds them hastily and then stands for months in the sunlight —a bundle of bare sticks soaked with a resin that will burn with fire, but will not evaporate with heat. The sangre de dragon (sometimes called sangre en grado) does the same thing. *The ocatilla.*

But Nature's most common device for the protection and preservation of her desert brood is to supply them with wonderful facilities for finding and sapping what moisture there is, and

Tap roots.

conserving it in tanks and reservoirs. The roots of the greasewood and the mesquite are almost as powerful as the arms of an octopus, and they are frequently three times the length of the bush or tree they support. They will bore their way through rotten granite to find a damp ledge almost as easily as a diamond drill; and they will pry rocks from their foundations as readily as the wistaria wrenches the ornamental wood-work from the roof of a porch. They are always thirsty and they are always running here and there in the search for moisture. A vertical section of their underground structure revealed by the cutting away of a river bank or wash is usually a great surprise. One marvels at the great network of roots required to support such a very little growth above ground.

Underground structure.

Yet this network serves a double purpose. It not only finds and gathers what moisture there is but stores it in its roots, feeding the top growth with it economically, not wastefully. It has no notion of sending too much moisture up to the sunlight and the air. Cut a twig and it will often appear very dry; cut a root and you will find it moist.

Feeding the top growth.

The storage reservoir below ground is not an unusual method of supplying water to the plant.

Many of the desert growths have it. Perhaps the most notable example of it is the wild gourd. This is little more than an enormous tap root that spreads out turnip-shaped and is in size often as large around as a man's body. It holds water in its pulpy tissue for months at a time, and while almost everything above ground is parched and dying the vines and leaves of the gourd, fed from the reservoir below, will go on growing and the flowers continue blooming with the most unruffled serenity. In the Sonora deserts there is a cactus or a bush (its name I have never heard) growing from a root that looks almost like a hornet's nest. This root is half-wood, half-vegetable, and is again a water reservoir like the root of the gourd.

Storage reservoirs below ground.

But there are reservoirs above ground quite as interesting as those below. The tall fluted column of the sahuaro, sometimes fifty feet high, is little more than an upright cistern for holding moisture. Its support within is a series of sticks arranged in cylindrical form and held together by some fibre, some tissue, and a great deal of saturated pulp. Drive a stick into it after a rain and it will run sap almost like the maguey from which the Indians distill mescal. All the cacti conserve water in their

Reservoirs above ground.

lobes or columns or at the base near the ground. So too the Spanish bayonets, the yuccas, the prickly pears and the chollas.

Many of the shrubs and trees like the sangre de dragon and the torote have enlarged or thickened barks to hold and supply water. If you cut them the sap runs readily. When it *Thickened barks.* congeals it forms a gum which heals over the wound and once more prevents evaporation. Existence for the plants would be impossible without such inventions. Plant life of every kind requires some moisture all the time. It is an error to suppose because they grow in the so-called " rainless desert " that therefore they exist without water. They gather and husband it during wet periods for use during dry *Gathering moisture.* periods, and in doing so they seem to display almost as much intelligence as a squirrel or an ant does in storing food for winter consumption.

Is Nature's task completed then when she has provided the plants with reservoirs of water and tap roots to pump for them ? By no means. How long would a tank of moisture exist in the *Attacks upon desert plants.* desert if unprotected from the desert animals ? The mule-deer lives here, and he can go for weeks without water, but he will take it every day if he can get it. And the coyote can run the hills indefinitely with little or no moisture; but he will eat a water melon, rind and all, and with great relish, when the opportunity offers. The sahuaro, the bisnaga, the cholla, and the pan-cake lobed prickly pear would have a short life and not a merry one if they were left to the mercy of the desert prowler. As it is they are *Browsing animals.* sometimes sadly worried about their roots by rabbits and in their lobes by the deer. It seems almost incredible but is not the less a fact, that deer and desert cattle will eat the cholla—fruit, stem, and trunk—though it bristles with spines that will draw blood from the human hand at the slightest touch.

Nature knows very well that the attack will come and so she provides her plants with various different defenses. The most common weapon which she gives them is the spine or thorn. Almost everything that grows has it and its different forms are many. They are all of them sharp as a needle and some of them have saw- *Weapons of defense.* edges that rip anything with which they come in contact. The grasses, and those plants akin to them like the yucca and the maguey, are often both saw-edged and spine-pointed. All the cacti have thorns, some straight, some barbed like a harpoon, some curved like a hook.

There are chollas that have a sheath covering the thorn—a scabbard to the sword—and when anything pushes against it the sheath is left sticking in the wound. The different forms of the bisnaga are little more than vegetable porcupines. They bristle with quills or have hook-shaped thorns that catch and hold the intruder.

The spine and thorn,

The sahuaro has not so many spines, but they are so arranged that you can hardly strike the cylinder without striking the thorns.

The cacti are defended better than the other growths because they have more to lose, and are consequently more subject to attack. And yet there is one notable exception. The crucifixion thorn is a bush or tree somewhat like the palo verde, except that it has no leaf. It is a

The crucifixion thorn.

thorn and little else. Each small twig runs out and ends in a sharp spike of which the branch is but the supporting shaft. It bears in August a small yellow flower but this grows out of the side of the spike. In fact the whole shrub seems created for no other purpose than the glorification of the thorn as a thorn.*

* It is said to be very scarce but I have found it growing along the Castle Creek region of Arizona, also at Kingman, Peach Springs, and further north. A stunted variety grows on the Mojave but it is not frequently seen on the Colorado.

Tree, bush, plant and grass—great and small alike—each has its sting for the intruder. You can hardly stoop to pick a desert flower or pull a bunch of small grass without being aware of a prickle on your hand. Nature seems to have provided a whole arsenal of defensive weapons for these poor starved plants of the desert. Not any of the lovely growths of the earth, like the lilies and the daffodils, are so well defended. And she has given them not only armor but a spirit of tenacity and stubbornness wherewith to carry on the struggle. Cut out the purslain and the iron weed from the garden walk, and it springs up again and again, contending for life. Put heat, drouth, and animal attack against the desert shrubs and they fight back like the higher forms of organic life. How typical they are of everything in and about the desert. There is but one word to describe it and that word—fierce—I shall have worn threadbare before I have finished these chapters.

The sting of flowers.

Fierceness of the plant.

We have not yet done with enumerating the defenses of these plants. The bushes like the greasewood and the sage have not the bulk of body to grow the thorn. They are too slight, too rambling in make-up. Besides their reservoirs are protected by being in their roots under

Odors and juices.

the ground. But Nature has not left their tops wholly at the mercy of the deer. Take the leaf of the sage and crush it in your hand. The odor is anything but pleasant. No animal except the jack-rabbit, no bird except the sage hen will eat it; and no human being will eat either the rabbit or the hen, if he can get anything else, because of the rank sage flavor. Rub the greasewood in your hand and it feels harsh and brittle. The resinous varnish of the leaves gives it a sticky feeling and a disagreeable odor again. Nothing on the desert will touch

Saps astringent and cathartic.

it. Cut or break a twig of the sangre de dragon and a red sap like blood runs out. Touch it to the tongue and it proves the most powerful of astringents. The Indians use it to cauterize bullet wounds. Again no animal will touch it. Half the plants on the desert put forth their leaves with impunity. They are not disturbed by either browsers or grazers. Some of them are poisonous, many of them are cathartic or emetic, nearly all of them are disagreeable to the taste.

So it seems with spines, thorns, barbs, resins, varnishes and odorous smells Nature has armed her desert own very effectually. And her expenditure of energy may seem singularly disproportionate to the result attained. The little vegetation that grows in the waste may not seem worth while, may seem insignificant compared with the great care bestowed upon it. But Nature does not think so. To her the cactus of the desert is just as important in its place as the arrowy pine on the mountain. She means that something shall grow and bear fruit after its kind even on the gravel beds of the Colorado; she means that the desert shall have its covering, scanty though it be, just the same as the well-watered lands of the tropics.

The expenditure of energy.

The desert covering.

But are they useful, these desert growths? Certainly they are; just as useful as the pine tree or the potato plant. To be sure, man cannot saw them into boards or cook them in a pot; but then Nature has other animals beside man to look after, other uses for her products than supporting human life. She toils and spins for all alike and man is not her special care. The desert vegetation answers her purposes and who shall say her purposes have ever been other than wise?

Use of desert plants.

Are they beautiful these plants and shrubs of the desert? Now just what do you mean by that word "beautiful"? Do you mean something of regular form, something smooth

Their beauty.

and pretty? Are you dragging into nature some remembrances of classic art; and are you looking for the Dionysius face, the Doryphorus form, among these trees and bushes? If so the desert will not furnish you too much of beauty. But if you mean something that has a distinct character, something appropriate to its setting, something admirably fitted to a designed end (as in art the peasants of Millet or the burghers of Rembrandt and Rodin), then the desert will show forth much that people nowadays are beginning to think beautiful. Mind you, perfect form and perfect

Beauty in character.

color are not to be despised; neither shall you despise perfect fitness and perfect character. The desert plants, every one of them, have very positive characters; and I am not certain but that many of them are interesting and beautiful even in form and color.

No doubt it is an acquired taste that leads one to admire greasewood and cactus; but can anyone be blind to the graceful form of the maguey, or better still, the yucca with its tall stalk rising like a shaft from a bowl and capped

Forms of the yucca and maguey.

at the top by nodding creamy flowers? On the mountains and the mesas the sahuaro is so common that perhaps we overlook its beauty of form ; yet its lines are as sinuous as those of a Moslem minaret, its flutings as perfect as those of a Doric column. Often and often you see it standing on a ledge of some rocky peak, like the lone shaft of a ruined temple on a Greek headland. And by way of contrast what could be more lovely than the waving lightness, the drooping gracefulness of the lluvia d'oro. The *The lluvia d'oro.* swaying tossing lluvia d'oro, well called the " shower of gold " ! It is one of the most beautiful of the desert trees with its white skin like the northern birch, its long needles like the pine, and the downward sweep of its branches like the willow. A strange wild tree that seems to shun all society, preferring to dwell like a hermit among the rocks. It roots itself in the fissures of broken granite and it seems at its happiest when it can let down its shower of gold over some precipice.

There are other tree forms, like the palo verde and the mesquite, that are not wanting in a native grace ; and yet it may as well be admitted that most of the trees and bushes are lacking in height, mass, and majesty. It is no place *Grotesque forms.* for large growths that reach up to the sun. The heat and drouth are too great and tend to make form angular and grotesque. But these very conditions that dwarf form perhaps enhance color by distorting it in an analogous manner. When plants are starved for water and grow in thin poor soil they often put on colors that are abnormal, even unhealthy. Because of starvation perhaps the little green of the desert is a sallow green ; and for the same reason the lobes of the prickly pear are pale-green, dull yellow, sad pink or livid mauve. The prickly pear seems to take all colors dependent upon the *Abnormal colors.* poverty, or the mineral character, of the ground where it grows. In that respect perhaps it is influenced in the same way as the parti-colored hydrangea of the eastern dooryard.

All the cacti are brilliant in the flowers they bear. The top of the bisnaga in summer is at first a mass of yellow, then bright orange, finally dark red. The sahuaro bears a purple flower, and the cholla, the ocatilla, the pitahaya come *Blossoms and flowers.* along with pink or gold or red or blue flowers. And again all the bushes and trees in summer put forth showers of color—graceful masses of petaled cups that look more like flowers grown in a meadow than blossoms grown on a tree. In June the palo verde is a great ball of yellow-gold, but there is a variety of it with a blue-green bark that grows a blossom almost like an

eastern violet. And down in Sonora one is daz-
zled by the splendor of the guyacan (or gual-
lacan) which throws out blossoms half-blue and
half-red. All the commoner growths like the
sage, the mesquite, the palo fierro, and the palo
blanco, are blossom bearers. In fact everything
that grows at all in the desert puts forth in season some bright little flag of color. In the *Many varieties.*
mass they make little show, but examined in
the part they are interesting because of their
nurture, their isolation, and their peculiarity
of form and color. The conditions of life have
perhaps contorted them, have paled or grayed
or flushed or made morbid their coloring ; but
they are all of them beautiful. Beautiful color
is usually unhealthy color as we have already
suggested.

Aside from the blossoms upon bush and tree
there are few bright petals shining in the desert. It is no place for flowers. They are too
delicate and are usually wanting in tap root
and armor. If they spring up they are soon
cut down by drouth or destroyed by animals.
Many tales are told of the flowers that grow on *Wild flowers.*
the waste after the rains, but I have not seen
them though I have seen the rains. There are
no lupins, phacelias, pentstemons, poppies, or

yellow violets. Occasionally one sees the wild verbena or patches of the evening primrose, or up in the swales the little baby blue-eye growing all alone, or perhaps the yellow mimulus ; but all told they do not make up a very strong

Salt-bush. contingent. The salt bush that looks the color of Scotch heather, out-bulks them all ; and yet is not conspicuously apparent. Higher up in the hills and along the mesas one often meets with many strange flowers, some fiery red and some with spines like the Canadian thistle ; but not down in the hot valleys of the desert.

The grasses. Nor are there many grasses of consequence aside from a small curled grass and the heavy sacaton that grow in bunches upon isolated portions of the desert. By "isolated" I mean that for some unknown reason there are tracts on the desert seemingly sacred to certain plants, some to cholla, some to yuccas, some to grease wood, some to sahuaros, some to sacaton grass. It seems to be a desert oddity that the vegetation does not mix or mingle to any great extent. There are seldom more than four or five kinds of growth to be found in one tract. It

The lichens. is even noticeable in the lichens. One mountain range will have all gray lichens on its northern walls, another range will have all orange lichens, and still another will be mottled by patches of coal-black lichens.

Strange growths of a strange land! Heat, drouth, and starvation gnawing at their vitals month in and month out; and yet how determined to live, how determined to fulfill their destiny! They keep fighting off the elements, the animals, the birds. Never by day or by night do they loose the armor or drop the spear point. And yet with all the struggle they serenely blossom in season, perpetuate their kinds, and hand down the struggle to the newer generation with no jot of vigor abated, no tittle of hope dissipated. Strange growths indeed! And yet strange, perhaps, only to us who have never known their untrumpeted history.

The continuous struggle.

CHAPTER IX

DESERT ANIMALS

THE life of the desert lives only by virtue of adapting itself to the conditions of the desert. Nature does not bend the elements to favor the plants and the animals; she makes the plants and the animals do the bending. The torote and the evening primrose must get used to heat, drouth, and a rocky bed; the coyote must learn to go without food and water for long periods. Even man, whose magnificent complacency leads him to think himself one of Nature's favorites, fares no better than a wild cat or an angle of cholla. He must endure the same heat, thirst, and hunger or perish. There is no other alternative.

Meeting desert requirements.

And so it happens that those things that can live in the desert become stamped after a time with a peculiar desert character. The struggle seems to develop in them special characteristics and make them, not different from their kind; but more positive, more insistent. The yucca

The peculiar desert character.

150

of the Mojave is the yucca of New Mexico and
Old Mexico but hardier; the wild cat of the
Colorado is the wild cat of Virginia but swifter,
more ferocious; the Yuma Indian is like the
Zuni or the Navajo but lanker, more sinewy,
more enduring. Father Garces, who passed
through here one hundred and twenty-five years
ago, records in his *Memoirs* more than once the
wonderful endurance of the desert Indians.
"The Jamajabs (a branch of the Yumas) endure hunger and thirst for four days," he writes
in one place. The tale is told that the Indians *Desert*
in the Coahuila Valley at the present day can *Indians.*
do substantially the same thing. And, too, it
is said that the Yumas have traveled from the
Colorado to the Pacific, across the desert on
foot, without any sustenance whatever. No
one, not to the desert born, could do such a
thing. Years of training in starvation, thirst
and exposure have produced a man almost as
hardy as the cactus, and just as distinctly a
type of the desert as the coyote.

But the Indian and the plant must have *some*
water. They cannot go without it indefinitely.
And just there the desert animals seem to fit *The*
their environment a little snugger than either *animals.*
plant or human. For, strange as it may ap-

pear, many of them get no water at all. There
are sections of the desert, fifty or more miles
square, where there is not a trace of water in
river, creek, arroyo or pocket, where there is
never a drop of dew falling; and where the two
or three showers of rain each year sink into the
Life without water. sand and are lost in half an hour after they
have fallen.   Yet that fifty-mile tract of sand
and rock supports its animal, reptile and insect
life just the same as a similar tract in Illinois
or Florida.   How the animals endure, how—
even on the theory of getting used to it—the
jack-rabbit, the ground squirrel, the rat, and
the gopher can live for months without even
the moisture from green vegetation, is one of
the mysteries. A mirror held to the nose of
a desert rabbit will show a moist breath-mark
on the glass.   The moisture came out of the
rabbit, is coming out of him every few sec-
onds of the day; and there is not a drop of
moisture going into him.   Evidently the ancient axiom: "Out of nothing, nothing comes"
is all wrong.

Endurance of the jack-rabbit.   It is said in answer that the jack-rabbit gets
moisture from roots, cactus-lobes and the like.
And the reply is that you find him where there
are no roots but greasewood and no cactus at

all. Besides there is no evidence from an examination of his stomach that he ever eats anything but dried grass, bark, and sage leaves. But if the matter is a trifle doubtful about the rabbit on account of his traveling capacities, there is no doubt whatever about the ground squirrels, the rock squirrels, and the prairie *Rock squirrels.* dogs. None of them ever gets more than a hundred yards from his hole in his life, except possibly when migrating. And the circuit about each hole is usually bare of everything except dried grass. There in no moisture to be had. The prairie dog is not found on the desert, but in Wyoming and Montana there are villages of them on the grass prairies, with no water, root, lobe, or leaf within miles of them. The old theory of the prairie dog digging his hole down *Prairie dogs and water.* to water has no basis in fact. Patience, a strong arm and a spade will get to the bottom of his burrow in half an hour.

All the desert animals know the meaning of a water famine, and even those that are pronounced water drinkers know how to get on with the minimum supply. The mule-deer whose cousin in the Adirondacks goes down to *Water famine.* water every night, lives in the desert mountains, month in and month out with nothing more watery to quench thirst than a lobe of the prickly pear or a joint of cholla. But he is naturally fond of green vegetation, and in the early morning he usually leaves the valley and climbs the mountains where with goats and mountain sheep be browses on the twigs of shrub and tree. The coyote likes water, too, but he puts up with sucking a nest of quail eggs, eating some mesquite beans, or at best absorbing the blood from some rabbit. The wild cat will go for weeks without more moisture than the blood of birds or lizards, and then perhaps, after long thirst, he will come to a water pocket in the rocks to lap only a handful, doing it with an angry snarling snap as though he disliked it and was drinking under compulsion. The gray wolf is too much of a traveler to depend upon any one locality. He will run fifty miles in a night and be back before morning. Whether he gets water or not is not possible to ascertain. The badger, the coon, and the bear are very seldom seen in the more arid regions. They are not strictly speaking desert animals because unfitted to endure desert hardships. They are naturally great eaters and sleepers, loving cool weather and their own fatness; and to that the desert is sharply opposed. There is nothing

Mule-deer browsing.

Coyotes and wild-cats living without water.

fat in the land of sand and cactus. Animal
life is lean and gaunt; if it sleeps at all it is with
one eye open ; and as for heat it cares very little about it. For the first law of the desert to
which animal life of every kind pays allegiance
is the law of endurance and abstinence. After
that requirement is fulfilled special needs produce the peculiar qualities and habits of the individual.

Lean, gaunt life.

Yet there is one quality more general than
special since almost everything possesses it, and
that is ferocity—fierceness. The strife is desperate ; the supply of food and moisture is
small, the animal is very hungry and thirsty.
What wonder then that there is the determi-
nation of the starving in all desert life ! Everything pursues or is pursued. Every muscle is
strung to the highest tension. The bounding
deer must get away ; the swift-following wolf
must not let him. The gray lizard dashes for
a ledge of rock like a flash of light ; but the
bayonet bill of the road runner must catch
him before he gets there. Neither can afford
to miss his mark. And that is perhaps the
reason why there is so much development in
special directions, so much fitness for a particular purpose, so much equipment for the

Fierceness of the animals.

Fitness for attack and escape.

doing or the avoiding of death. Because the wild-cat cannot afford to miss his quarry, therefore is he made a something that seldom does miss.

The wild-cat.

The description of the lion as "a jaw on four paws" will fit the wild-cat very well—only he is a jaw on two paws. The hind legs are insignificant compared with the front ones, and the body back of the shoulders is lean, lank, slight, but withal muscular and sinewy. The head is bushy, heavy, and square, the neck and shoulders are massive, the forelegs and paws so large that they look to belong to some other animal. The ears are small yet sensitive enough to catch the least noise, the nose is acute, the eyes are like great mirrors, the teeth like points of steel. In fact the whole animal is little more than a machine for dragging down and devouring prey. That and the protection of his breed are his only missions on earth. He is the same creeping, snarling beast that one finds in the mountains of California, but the desert animal is larger and stronger. He sneaks upon a band of quail or a rabbit with greater caution, and

The spring of the cat.

when he springs and strikes it is with greater certainty. The enormous paws pin the game to the earth, and the sharp teeth cut through like knives. It is not more than once in two or three days that a meal comes within reach and he has no notion of allowing it to get away.

The panther, or as he is more commonly called, the mountain lion, is no such square-built mass of muscle, no such bundle of energy as the wild-cat, though much longer and larger. The figure is wiry and serpentine, and has all the action and grace of the tiger. It is pre-eminently a figure for crouching, sneaking, springing, and dragging down. His struggle-for-life is perhaps not so desperate as that of the cat because he lives high up in the desert mountains where game is more plentiful; but he is a very good struggler for all that. Occasionally one hears his cry in the night (a cry that stops the yelp of the coyote very quickly and sets the ears of the jack-rabbit a-trembling) but he is seldom seen unless sought for. Even then the seeker does not usually care to look for him, or at him too long. He has the tiger eye, and his jaw and claw are too powerful to be trifled with. He will not attack one unless at bay or wounded; but as a mountain prowler he is the terror of the young deer, the mountain sheep, and the rabbit family.

The mountain lion.

Habits of the mountain lion.

One sees the gray wolf but little oftener than the mountain lion. Sometimes in the very

The gray wolf.

early morning you may catch a glimpse of him
sneaking up a mountain canyon, but he usually
keeps out of sight. His size is great for a wolf
—sometimes over six feet from nose to tail tip
—but it lies mostly in length and bulk. He does
not stand high on his feet and yet is a swift and
long-winded runner. In this and in his strength
of jaw lies his special equipment. He is not
very cunning but he takes up and follows a
trail, and runs the game to earth with considerable perseverance. I have never seen anything
but his footprints on the desert. Usually he
keeps well up in the mountains and comes down
on the plains only at night. He prefers prairie
or table-land country, with adjacent stock
Home of the wolf. ranges, to the desert, because there the hunting
is not difficult. Sheep, calves, and pigs he will
eat with some relish, but his favorite game is the
young colt. He runs all his game and catches
it as it runs like the true wolf that he is. Sometimes he hunts in packs of half a dozen, but if
there is no companionship he does not hesitate
to hunt alone.

The coyote. The prairie wolf or coyote is not at all like
the gray wolf. He seldom runs after things,
though he does a good deal of running away
from them. And he is a fairly good runner too.

But he does not win his living by his courage.
His special gift is not the muscular energy that
crushes at a blow ; nor the great strength that
follows and tires and finally drags down. Nature designed him with the wolf form and instinct, but gave him something of the cleverness of the fox. It is by cunning and an
obliging stomach that the coyote is enabled to
eke out a living. He is cunning enough to
know, for instance, that you cannot see him on
a desert background as long as he does not
move ; so he sits still at times for many minutes, watching you from some little knoll. As
long as he is motionless your eyes pass over him
as a patch of sand or a weathered rock. When
he starts to move, it is with some deliberation.
He prefers a dog-trot and often several shots
from your rifle will not stir him into a run. He
slips along easily and gracefully—a lean, hungry-
looking wretch with all the insolence of a hood-
lum and all the shrewdness of a thief. He requires just such qualities together with a keen
nose, good eyes and ears, and some swiftness of
dash to make a living. The desert bill of fare
is not all that a wolf could desire ; but the coyote
is not very particular. Everything is food that
comes to his jaws. He likes rabbit meat, but

Cleverness of the coyote.

does not often get it. For desert rabbits do not go to sleep with both eyes shut. Failing the rabbit he snuffs out birds and their nests, *His subsistence.* trails up anything sick or wounded, and in emergencies runs down and devours a lizard. If animal food is scarce he turns his attention to vegetation, eats prickly pears and mesquite beans; and up in the mountains he stands on his hind legs and gathers choke cherries and manzanitas. With such precarious living he becomes gaunt, leathery, muscled with whip-cord. There is a meagreness and a scantiness about him; his coarse coat of hair is sun-scorched, his whole appearance is arid, dusty, sandy. There is no other animal so thoroughly typical of the desert. *His background.* He belongs there, skulking along the arroyos and washes just as a horned toad belongs under a granite bowlder. That he can live there at all is due to Nature's gift to him of all-around cleverness.

The fox The fox is usually accounted the epitome of animal cunning, but here in the desert he is not frequently seen and is usually thought less clever than the coyote. He prefers the foot-hills and the cover of dense chaparral where he preys upon birds, smells out the nest of the valley quail, catches a wood-rat; or, if hard pushed to it, makes a meal of crickets and grass-hoppers. But even at this he is not more facile than the coyote. Nor can he surpass the coyote in robbing a hen-roost and keeping out of a trap while doing it. He cuts no important fig-ure on the desert and, indeed, he is hardly a desert animal though sometimes found there. The conditions of existence are too severe for him. The strength of the cat, the legs of the wolf, and the stomach of the coyote are not his; and so he prowls nearer civilization and takes more risk for an easier life.

And the prey, what of the prey! The ani- *The prey.*
mals of the desert that furnish food for the meat eaters like the wolf and the cat—the ani-mals that cannot fight back or at least wage un-equal warfare—are they left hopelessly and help-lessly at the mercy of the destroyers? Not so. Nature endows them and protects them as best she can. Every one of them has some device to baffle or trick the enemy. Even the poor little horned toad, that has only his not too thick skin to save him, can slightly change the color of that skin to suit the bowlder he is flattened *Devices for escape.* upon so that the keenest eye would pass him over unnoticed. The jack-rabbit cannot change his skin, but he knows many devices whereby he

contrives to save it. Lying in his form at the root of some bush or cactus he is not easily seen. He crouches low and the gray of his fur fits into the sand imperceptibly. You do not see him but he sees you. His eyes never close; *Senses of the rabbit.* they are always watching. Look at them closely as he lies dead before you and how large and protruding they are ! In the life they see everything that moves. And if his eyes fail him, perhaps his ears will not. He was named the jackass-rabbit because of his long ears ; and the length of them is in exact proportion to their acuteness of hearing. No footstep escapes them. They are natural megaphones for the reception of sound. It can hardly be doubted that his nose is just as acute as his eyes and his ears. So that all told he is not an animal easily caught napping.

And if the jack-rabbit's senses fail him, has he no other resource ? Certainly, yes ; that is if he is not captured. In proportion to his size he has the strongest hind legs of anything on *Speed of the jack-rabbit.* the desert. In this respect he is almost like a kangaroo. When he starts running and begins with his long bound, there is nothing that can overtake him except a trained greyhound. He ricochets from knoll to knoll like a bounding ball, and as he crosses ahead of you perhaps you think he is not moving very fast. But shoot at him and see how far behind him your rifle ball strikes the dust. No coyote or wolf is foolish enough to chase him or ever try to run him down. His endurance is quite as good as his speed. It makes no difference about his not drinking water and that all his energy comes from bark and dry grass. He keeps right on running ; over stones, through cactus, down a canyon, up a mountain. For keen senses and swift legs he is the desert type as emphatically as the coyote that is forever prowling on his track.

His endurance.

The little " cotton-tail " rabbit is not perhaps so well provided for as the jack-rabbit ; but then he does not live in the open and is not so exposed to attack. He hides in brush, weeds, or grass ; and when startled makes a quick dash for a hole in the ground or a ledge of rock. His legs are good for a short distance, and his senses are acute ; but the wild-cat or the coyote catches him at last. The continuance of his species lies in prolific breeding. The wild-cat, too, catches a good many gophers, rats, mice, and squirrels. The squirrels are many in kind and beautiful in their forms and colorings. One

The "cotton-tail."

can hardly count them all—squirrels with long tails and short tails and no tails; squirrels yellow, brown, gray, blue, and slate-colored. They live in the rocks about the bases of the desert mountains; and eventually they fall a prey to the wild-cat who watches for them just as the domestic cat watches for the house rat. Their only safeguard is their energetic way of darting into a hole. For all their sharp noses and ears they are foolish little folk and will keep poking their heads out to see what is going on.

Squirrels and gophers.

But for acute senses, swift legs, and powerful endurance nothing can surpass the antelope. He is rarely seen to-day (more's the pity!); but only a few years ago there were quite a number of them on the Sonora edge of the Colorado Desert. Usually they prefer the higher mesas where the land is grass-grown and the view is unobstructed; but they have been known to come far down into the desert. And the antelope is very well fitted for the sandy waste. The lack of water does not bother him, he can eat anything that grows in grass or bush; and he can keep from being eaten about as cleverly as any of the deer tribe. His eye alone is a marvel of development. It protrudes from the socket

The desert antelope.

His eyes.

—bulges out almost like the end of an egg—
and if there were corners on the desert mesas
I believe that eye could see around them. He
cannot be approached in any direction without
seeing what is going on; but he may be still-
hunted and shot from behind crag or cover.

His curiosity is usually the death of him, because he will persist in standing still and looking at things; but his senses almost always give
him fair warning. His nose and ears are just *His nose and ears.*
as acute as his eyes. And how he can run!
His legs seem to open and shut like the blades
of a pocket-knife, so leisurely, so apparently
effortless. But how they do take him over the
ground! With one leg shot from under him
he runs pretty nearly as fast as before. A
tougher, more wiry, more beautiful animal was
never created. Perhaps that is the reason why
every man's hand has been raised against him
until now his breed is almost extinct. He was
well fitted to survive on the desert mesas and
the upland plains—a fine type of swiftness and *His swiftness.*
endurance—but Nature in her economy never
reckoned with the magazine rifle nor the greed
of the individual who calls himself a sports-
man.

The mule-deer with his large ears, long muzzle and keen eyes, is almost as well provided for as the antelope. He has survived the antelope possibly because he does not live in the open country. He haunts the brush and the rock cover of the gorge and the mountain side. There in the heavy chaparral he will skulk and hide while you may pass within a few feet of him. If he sees that he is discovered he can make a dash up or down the mountain in a way that astonishes. Stones, sticks, and brush have no terror for him. He jumps over them or smashes through them. He will bound across a talus of broken porphyry that will cut the toughest boots to pieces, striking all four feet with every bound, and yet not ruffle the hair around his dew claws; or he will dash through a tough dry chaparral at full speed without receiving a scrape or a cut of any kind.

The speed he attains on such ground astonishes again. His feet seem to strike rubber instead of stone; for he bounds like a ball, describes a quarter circle, and bounds again. The magazine of your rifle may be emptied at him; and still he may go on, gayly cutting quarter circles, until he disappears over the ridge. He is one of the hardiest of the desert progeny. The lack of water affects him little. He browses and gets fat on twigs and leaves that seem to have as little nutriment about them as a telegraph-pole; and he lies down on a bed of stones as upon a bed of roses. He is as tough as the goats and sheep that keep well up on the high mountain ridges; and in cleverness is perhaps superior to the antelope. But oftentimes he will turn around to have a last look, and therein lies his undoing. In Sonora there is found a dwarf deer—a foolish if pretty little creature—and along river-beds the white-tailed deer is occasionally seen; but these deer with the goats and the sheep hardly belong to the desert, though living upon its confines. *Habits of the desert-deer.* *The white-tail.*

In fact, none of the far-travelling animals lives right down in the desert gravel-beds continuously. They go there at night or in the early morning, but in the daytime they are usually found in the neighboring hills. The rabbits, rats, and squirrels, if undisturbed, will usually stay upon the flat ground; and there is also another variety of desert life that does not wander far from the sand and the rocks. I mean the reptiles. They are not as a class swift in flight, nor over-clever in sense, nor cunning in devices. Nor have they sufficient strength to grapple and fight with the larger animals. It *The reptiles.*

would seem as though Nature had brought them into the desert only half made-up—a prey to every beast and bird. But no; they are given the most deadly weapon of defence of all —poison. Almost all of the reptiles have poison about them in fang or sting. We are accustomed to label them " poisonous " or "not poisonous," as they kill or do not kill a human being; but that is not the proper criterion by which to judge. The bite of the trap-door spider will not seriously affect a man, but it will kill a lizard in a few minutes. In proportion to his size the common red ant of the desert is more poisonous than the rattlesnake. It is reiterated with much positiveness that a swarm of these ants have been known to kill men. There is, however, only one reptile on the desert that humanity need greatly fear on account of his poison and that is the rattlesnake. There are several varieties called in local parlance "side-winders," "ground rattlers," and the like; but the ordinary spotted, brown, or yellow rattlesnake is the type. He is not a pleasant creature, but then he is not often met with. In travelling many hundreds of miles on the desert I never encountered more than half a dozen.

Poison of reptiles.

The fang and sting.

The rattle is indescribable, but a person will know it the first time he hears it. It is something between a buzz and a burr, and can cause a cold perspiration in a minute fraction of time. The snake is very slow in getting ready to strike, in fact sluggish ; but once the head shoots out, it does so with the swiftness of an arrow. Nothing except the road-runner can dodge it. The poison is deadly if the fang has entered a vein or a fleshy portion of the body where the flow of blood to the heart is free. If struck on the hand or foot, the man may recover, because the circulation there is slow and the heart has time to repel the attack. Every animal on the desert knows just how venomous is that poison. Even your dog knows it by instinct. He may shake and kill garter-snakes, but he will not touch the rattlesnake.

The rattle-snake.

Effect of the poison.

All of the spider family are poisonous and you can find almost every one of them on the desert. The most sharp-witted of the family is the trap-door spider—the name coming from the door which he hinges and fastens over the entrance of his hole in the ground. The tarantula is simply an overgrown spider, very heavy in weight, and inclined to be slow and stupid in action. He is a ferocious-looking wretch

Spiders and tarantulas.

and has a ferocious bite. It makes an ugly wound and is deadly enough to small animals. The scorpion has the reputation of being very venomous; but his sting on the hand amounts to little more than that of an ordinary wasp.

Nor is the long-bodied, many-legged, rather graceful centipede so great a poison-carrier as has been alleged. They are all of them poisonous, but in varying degrees. Doubtless the (to us) harmless horned toads and the swifts have for their enemies some venom in store.

The lizards are many in variety, and their colors are often very beautiful in grays, yellows, reds, blues, and indigoes. The Gila monster belongs to their family, though he is much larger. The look of him is very forbidding and he has an ugly way of hissing at you; but just how venomous he is I do not know. Very likely there is some poison about him, though this has been denied. It would seem that everything that cannot stand or run or hide must be defended somehow. Even the poor little skunk when he comes to live on the desert develops poisoned teeth and his bite produces what is called hydrophobia. The truth about the hydrophobia skunk is, I imagine, that he is an eater of carrion; and when he bites a person he is likely to produce blood-poisoning, which is miscalled hydrophobia.

Taking them for all in all, they seem like a precious pack of cutthroats, these beasts and reptiles of the desert. Perhaps there never was a life so nurtured in violence, so tutored in attack and defence as this. The warfare is continuous from the birth to the death. Everything must fight, fly, feint, or use poison ; and every slayer eventually becomes a victim. What a murderous brood for Nature to bring forth ! And what a place she has chosen in which to breed them ! Not only the struggle among themselves, but the struggle with the land, the elements — the eternal fighting with heat, drouth, and famine. What else but fierceness and savagery could come out of such conditions ? *The cutthroat band.* *The eternal struggle.*

But, after all, is there not something in the sheer brute courage that endures, worthy of our admiration ? These animals have made the best out of the worst, and their struggle has given them a physical character which is, shall we not say, beautiful ? Perhaps you shudder at the thought of a panther dragging down a deer— one enormous paw over the deer's muzzle, one on his neck, and the strain of all the back mus- *Brute courage.*

cles coming into play. But was not that the purpose for which the panther was designed ? As a living machine how wonderfully he works! Look at the same subject done in bronze by Barye and you will see what a revelation of *Brute character.* character the great statuary thought it. Look, too, at Barye's wolf and fox, look at the lions of Géricault, and the tigers and serpents of Delacroix ; and with all the jaw and poison of them how beautiful they are !

You will say they are made beautiful through the art of the artists, and that is partly true ; but we are seeing only what the artists saw. And how did they come to choose such subjects ? Why, simply because they recognized that for art there is no such thing as nobility or vulgarity of subject. Everything may be fit if *Beauty in character.* it possesses character. The beautiful is the characteristic—the large, full-bodied, well-expressed truth of character. At least that is one very positive phase of beauty.

Even the classic idea of beauty, which regards only the graceful in form or movement *Graceful forms of animals.* or the sensuous in color, finds types among these desert inhabitants. The dullest person in the arts could not but see fine form and proportion in the panther, graceful movement in the antelope, and charm of color in all the pretty rock squirrels. For myself, being somewhat prejudiced in favor of this drear waste and its savage progeny, I may confess to having watched the flowing movements of snakes, their coil and rattle and strike, many times and with great pleasure ; to having stretched myself for hours upon granite bowlders while following the play of indigo lizards in the sand ; to having traced with surprise the slightly changing skin of the horned toad produced by the reflection of different colors held near him. I may also confess that common as is the jack-rabbit he never bursts away in speed before me without being followed by my wonder at his graceful mystery of motion ; that the crawl of a wild-cat upon game is something that arrests and fascinates by its masterful skill ; and that even that desert tramp, the coyote, is entitled to admiration for the graceful way he can slip through patches of cactus. The fault is not in the subject. It is not vulgar or ugly. The trouble is that we perhaps have not the proper angle of vision. If we understood all, we should admire all.

Colors of lizards.

Mystery of motion.

CHAPTER X

WINGED LIFE

The first day's walk.

THE desert's secrets of life and growth and death are not to be read at a glance. The first day's walk is usually a disappointment. You see little more than a desolate waste. The light of the blue sky, the subtle color of the air, the roll of the valleys, the heave of the mountains do not reveal themselves at once. The vegetation you think looks like a thin covering of dry sticks. And as for the animals, the birds —the living things on the desert—they are not apparent at all.

But the casual stroll does not bring you to the end of the desert's resources. You may perhaps walk for a whole day and see not a beast or a bird of any description. Yet they are here.

Tracks in the sand.

Even in the lava-beds where not even cactus will grow, and where to all appearance there is no life whatever, you may see tracks in the sand where quail and road-runners and linnets have been running about in search of food. There

174

are tracks, too, of the coyote and the wild-cat—
tracks following tracks. The animals and the
birds belong to the desert or the neighboring
mountains ; but they are not always on view.
You meet with them only in the early morning
and evening when they are moving about. In
the middle of the day they are in the shadow of
bush or rock or lying in some cut bank or cave
—keeping out of the direct rays of the sun.
The birds are not very numerous even when *Scarcity of birds.*
they come forth. They prefer places that afford
better cover. And yet as you make a memo-
randum of each new bird you see you are surprised after a time to find how many are the
varieties.

And the surprise grows when you think of
the dangers and hardships that continually har-
ass bird-life here in the desert. It may be *Dangers of bird-life.*
fancied perhaps that the bird is exempt from
danger because he has wings to carry him out
of the reach of the animals ; but we forget that
he has enemies of his own kind in the air. And
if he avoids the hawks by day, how shall he
avoid the owls by night ? Where at night shall *No cover for protection.*
he go for protection ? There are no broad-
leaved trees to offer a refuge—in fact few trees
of any sort. The bushes are not so high that

a coyote cannot reach to their top at a jump ;
nor are the spines and ledges of rock in the
mountains so steep that a wild-cat cannot climb
up them.

No ; the bird is subject to the same dangers
as the animals and the plants. Something is
forever on his trail. He must always be on
guard. And the food problem, ever of vital
interest to bird-life, bothers him just as much
as it does the coyote. There is little for him
to eat and nothing for him to drink ; and hardly a resting-place for the sole of his foot. Besides, it would seem as though he should be af-
fected by the intense heat more than he is in
reality. Humanity at times has difficulty in
withstanding this heat, for though it is not
suffocating, it parches the mouth and dries up
the blood so rapidly that if water is not attain-
able the effect is soon apparent. The animals
—that is, the wild ones—are never fazed by it ;
but the domestic horse, dog, and cow yield to
it almost as readily as a man. And men and
animals are all of low-blood temperature—a
man's normal temperature being about 98 F.
But what of the bird in his coat of feathers
which may add to or detract from his warmth ?
What is his normal temperature ? It varies

The food problem.

The heat and drouth again.

with the species, so far as I can ascertain by ex-
periment, from 112 to 120 F.   Consider that
blood temperature in connection with a sur-
rounding air varying from 100 to 125 F. !   It   *A bird's temperature.*
would seem impossible for any life to support
it.   One may well wonder what strange wings
beat this glowing air, what bird-life lives in this
fiery waste !

Yet the desert-birds look not very different
from their cousins of the woods and streams
except that they are thinner, more subdued in
color, somewhat more alert.   They are very
pretty, very innocent-looking birds.   But we   *Innocent-looking birds with savage instincts.*
may be sure that living here in the desert, en-
during its hardships and participating in its incessant struggle for life and for the species, they
have just the same savage instincts as the plants
and the animals.   The sprightliness and the
color may suggest harmlessness ; but the eye,
the beak, the claw are designed for destruction.
The road-runner is one of the mildest-looking   *The road-runner.*
and most graceful birds of the desert, but the
spring of the wild-cat to crush down a rabbit is
not more fierce than the snap of the bird's beak
as he tosses a luckless lizard.   He is the only
thing on the desert that has the temerity to
fight a rattlesnake.   It is said that he kills the

snake, but as to that I am not able to give evidence.

And it is not alone the bird of prey—not alone the road-runners, the eagles, the vultures, the hawks, and the owls that are savage of mood. Every little wisp of energy that carries a bunch of feathers is endowed with the same spirit. The downward swoop of the cactus wren upon a butterfly and the snip of his little scissors bill, the dash after insects of the fly-catchers, vireos, swallows, bats, and whippoor-wills are just as murderous in kind as the blow of the condor and the vice-like clutch of his talons as they sink into the back of a rabbit. Skill and strength in the chase are absolutely necessary in a desert where food is so scarce, and in proportion the little birds have these qualities in common with the great.

Wrens and fly-catchers.

And naturally, as in the case of the animals, the skill and the strength develop along the line of the bird's needs, producing that quality of character, that fitness for the work cut out for him, to which we have so often referred. There are birds that belong almost solely to the kingdom of the air—birds like the condor, the vulture, and the eagle. Upon the ground they move awkwardly, not having better feet to

Development of special characteristics.

walk with than ducks and geese. The talons are too much developed for walking. When they rise from the ground they do it heavily and with quick flapping wings. Not until they are fairly started in the upper air do they show what wonderful wing-power they possess.

Birds of the air.

The common brown-black vulture or turkey buzzard is the type of all the wheelers and sailers. The "soaring eagle" of poetry is something of a goose beside him. For the wings of the vulture bear him through wind, sun, and heat, hour after hour, without a pause. To see him circling as he hunts down a mountain range a hundred miles or more, one might think that the abnormal breast-muscles never grew weary. He goes over every foot of the ground with his eyes and at the same time watches every other vulture in the sky. Let one of his fellows stop circling and drop earthward on a long incline, and immediately he is followed by all the black crew. They know instantly that something has been discovered. But often the hunt is in vain, and then for whole days at a time those motionless wings bear their burden apparently without fatigue. With no food perhaps for a fortnight and

The brown-black vulture.

The vulture hunting.

never any water, that spare rack of muscles sails the air with as little effort as floating thistle-down. No one knows just how it is done. In blow or calm, against the wind or with it, high in the blue or low over the ground, any place, anywhere, and under any circumstances those wings cut through the air almost like sunlight. You can hear a whizz like the flight of arrows as the bird passes close over your head; but you cannot see the slightest motion in the feathers.

The vulture sailing.

The hot, thin air of the desert would seem a less favorable air for sailing than the moister atmosphere of the south; but the vulture of the tropics is not the equal of the desert-bird. He is heavier, lazier, and more stupid—possibly because better fed. There are several varieties in the family, the chief variants being the one with white tipped wings and the one with a white eagle-like head. Neither of them is as good on the wing as the black species, though none of them is to be despised. Even the ordinary carrion crow of the desert is an expert sailer compared with any of the crow family to be found elsewhere. The exigencies of the situation seem to require wings developed for long-distance flights; and the vultures, the crows,

The southern buzzard.

The crow.

the eagles, the hawks, all respond after their individual fashions.

The condor is perhaps the vulture's peer in the matter of sailing. He belongs to the vulture family, though very much larger than any of its members, sometimes measuring fifteen feet across the wings and weighing forty pounds. He is the largest bird on the continent. At the present time he is occasionally seen wheeling high in air like a mere insect in the great blue dome. It is said that he soars as high as twentyfive thousand feet above the earth. But to-day he sails alone and his tribe has grown less year by year. With the eagles he keeps well up in the high sierras and builds a nest on the inaccessible peaks or along the steep escarpments. He belongs to the desert only because it is one of his hunting-grounds. *The great condor.*

This may be said of the eagles and the hawks. They hunt the desert by day, but go home to the mountains at night. The owls are somewhat different, not being given to long flight. The deep caves or wind-worn recesses under mountain ledges furnish them abiding-places. These caves also send forth at dusk a full complement of bats that seem not different from the ordinary Eastern bats. The burrowing *The eagles and hawks.*

Bats and owls.

owl is perhaps misnamed, though not misplaced. There is no evidence whatever, that I have ever seen or heard, to show that he burrows. What happens is that he crawls into some hole that is already burrowed instead of a cave or recess in the rocks. A prairie-dog or badger hole is his preference. That the place has inhabitants, including the tarantula and (it is said) the rattlesnake, does not bother the owl. He walks in with his mate and speedily makes himself at home. How the different families get on together can be imagined by one person as well as

The burrowing owl.

by another. They do not seem to pay any attention to each other so far as I have observed. Ordinarily the desert animals, birds, and reptiles agree to no such truce. They are at war from the start. I do not know that the owls, the bats, the night-hawks have any special equipment for carrying on their part of the war. Sometimes I have fancied they had larger eyes than is usual with their kinds outside of the desert ; but I have no proof of this. Perhaps it is like the speculation as to whether the buzzard sees or scents the carrion that he discovers so readily—hardly amenable to proof.

All of the air-birds are strikingly developed in the wings and equally undeveloped in the

feet, while all the ground-birds of the desert
are just the reverse of this—that is, deficient in
wings but strong of foot and leg. The road-
runner, or as he is sometimes called the chap-
arralcock, is a notable instance of this. He is
a lizard-eater, and in order to eat he must first
catch his lizard. Now this is by no means an
easy task. The ordinary gray, brown, or yellow lizard is the swiftest dodger and darter
there is in the sand, and even in straight-line
running he will travel too fast for an ordinary
dog to catch him. His facility, too, in dashing
up, over, and under bowlders is not to be under-
estimated. The road-runner's task then is not
an easy one, and yet he seems to accomplish it
easily. There is no great effort about his pursuit and yet he generally manages to catch the
lizard. It is because his legs are specially constructed for running, and his head, neck, and
beak for darting. His wings are of little use.
When chased by a dog he will finally take to
them, but only for about fifty yards. Then he
drops to the ground and starts on foot again.
He will run away from a man, and sometimes
even a horse cannot keep up with him. Oddly
enough, he seems always to run a little side-
ways. The long tail (used as a rudder) is car-

ried a little to the right or the left and gives this impression. When frightened, his top-knot is raised like that of the pheasant, and he often

The vicious beak.

runs with his beak open. It is a most vicious beak for all that it looks not more blood-thirsty than that of the crow. It snaps through a scorpion or a centipede like a pair of sheep-shearers. And with all his energy and strength the road-runner weighs only about a pound. He is a long-geared bird, but not actually any larger than a pigeon.

The desert-quail.

The blue valley-quail—whether of Arizona or California breeding—is quite as strong of leg as the road-runner, though not perhaps so swift. He does not care much about using his wings ; and at best they are not better than the rather poor average of quails' wings. By that I mean that all quails rise from cover with a great roar and bustle, and they fly very fast for a short distance ; but they are soon down upon the ground, running and hiding. The flight of the quail, too, is straight ahead. It is not possible for him to rise up over five hundred feet of canyon wall, for instance, and even on an ordinary mountain side he takes several flights be-

Wings of the quail.

fore he reaches the summit. The wings are not muscled like the legs, and that is because the quail is a ground-bird. He gets his food there and spends most of his time there. In the East Bob White always roosts upon the ground, but the desert-quail is usually too clever to trust himself in such an exposed place. He will travel miles to get into a cotton-wood tree at dusk, and if there is water near at hand so much the better. He dearly loves the water and the tree, but if he cannot get them he accepts the situation philosophically and goes to sleep on a high ledge of rock with water perhaps in his thought but not in his crop.

Travelling for water.

Thanks to his capacity for travelling, the quail usually manages to get enough of small seeds and insects to keep himself alive. He is a great roamer—in the course of a day travelling over many miles of country—and his quest is always food. He likes to be among the great bowlders that lie along the bases of the mountains ; and when disturbed he flies and jumps from rock to rock, much to the discouragement of the coyote that happens to be the disturber. When forced to rise he flies perhaps for a hundred yards or more and then drops and begins running. In the spring he mates, raises a brood, and teaches the young ones the gentle art of running. In the fall he and his family

Habits of quail.

of a dozen or sixteen join with other families
to make a great covey of several hundred, or in
the old days before the market-hunters came,
several thousand.   And they all run.   The
bottom of the quail's foot is always itching for
the ground ; and he seems never so happy as
when leaving the enemy far behind him.   His

His strong legs.

little legs take him through the brush so fast
that you cannot keep up with him.   Every
muscle in him is as tough as a watch-spring.
You may wound him, but you have not yet got
him.   He will creep into some cactus patch or
crawl down a snake-hole—elude you in some
way—and in the end die game just out of your
reach.

There are few trees upon the desert and few
bushes of any size ; yet there are birds of the

Bush-birds.

tree and the bush here just as there are birds
of the air and the ground.   The most of them
seem the same kind of linnets, sparrows, and
thrushes that are seen along the California
coast ; though probably they have some peculiar
desert characteristic.   I cannot see any difference between the little woodpeckers here and
the woodpeckers elsewhere ; yet this desert variety flies from sahuaro to sahuaro, alights on
the spiny trunk with a little thump, and im-

mediately begins hitching himself up through the worst imaginable rows of needles just as though he were climbing a plain pine-tree. The ordinary turtle-dove with his red pigeon-feet alights on the top of the same sahuaro, the wren bores holes in it and makes a nest within the cylinder; and the dwarf thrush dashes in and out of tangled thickets of cholla all day long, and yet none of them suffers any injury. It seems incredible that birds not accustomed to the desert could do such things. *The wood-peckers and cactus.*

Possibly, too, these bush-birds — insect-devourers most of them—have some special faculty for catching their prey, though I have not been able to discover it. The fly-catchers, the mocking-birds, the finches, in a land of plenty are quick enough in breaking the back of a butterfly or beetle, and any extra energy would seem superfluous. Still there is no telling what fine extra stimulus lies in an empty crop. And crops are usually empty on the desert. Even the little humming-bird has difficulty in picking a living. In blossom time he is, of course, in fine condition, but I have seen him dashing about in the fall when nothing at all was in bloom, and evidently none the worse for some starvation. He is a swifter flyer than the or- *Finches and mocking-birds.* *The humming-bird.*

dinary bird and is also duller in coloring, but in other respects he seems not different. He breeds on the desert, building his nest in the pitahaya; and he and his mate then have a standing quarrel with their neighbors for the rest of the summer. There is not in the whole feathered tribe a more quarrelsome scrap of vivacity than the humming-bird.

Doves and grosbeaks.

The dwarf dove common to Sonora, the oven-bird, the red grosbeak, and many other of the smaller birds known to civilization, are found on the desert; but apparently with no special faculty for overcoming its hardships. This is due perhaps to the fact that they are not always there — are not exclusively desert-birds. Nor do any of the migratory birds belong to the desert, though they stop here for weeks at a time in their flights north or south. At almost any season of the year one sees the cow-blackbird and the smaller crow-blackbird. The mocking-bird comes only in the spring and fall, and the lark in early summer. The lark looks precisely like the Eastern bird, but his note is changed; whereas the flicker has changed the color under his wings from yellow to pink, but not his note. The robin is no whit different from the front-lawn robin of

The lark and flicker.

our childhood ; and the bobolink rising from
salt-bush and yucca, singing as he rises, is the
bobolink of ancient days.   At times there are
troops of magpies that come and go across the *Jays and*
waste, and at other times troops of blue-jays. *magpies.*
And high in air through the warmth of spring
and the cold of autumn there are great flocks
of ducks, geese, brant, divers, shags, willet, *Water-fowl.*
curlew, swinging along silently to the southern
or northern waterways.   They seldom pause,
even when following the Colorado River, unless
in need of water.   On the mesas and uplands
one sometimes sees a group of sand-hill cranes
walking about and indulging in a crazy dance
peculiarly their own, but the sight is no longer a common one.

   And again the prey—what of the prey ? Has
Nature left the beetles, the bugs, the worms, *Beetles and*
the bees, completely at the pleasure of the bird's *worms.*
beak ? No ; not completely, though it must
be acknowledged that she has not provided
much defensive armor for them individually.
She incases her beautiful blue and yellow
beetles in hard shells that other insects cannot
break through, but they are flimsy defences
against the mocking-bird.   To bugs and worms
and bees she gives perhaps a sting, deadly

enough when thrust into a spider, but useless again when used in defence against a cactus-thrush. And this is where Nature shows her absolute indifference to the life or the death of the individual. She allows the bugs and beetles to be slaughtered like the mackerel in the sea. But she is a little more careful about preserving the species. And how does she do this without preserving the individual ? Why, simply by increasing the number of individuals, by breed, by fertility, by multiplicity. Thousands are annually slaughtered ; yes, but thousands are annually bred. What matter about their lives or deaths provided they do not increase or decrease as a species !

Fighting destruction by breed.

The insects on the desert are mere flashes of life—pin-points of energy—but not without purpose and not without beauty. The beasts and the birds may be bleached brown or gray by the sun ; but the insects are many of them as gay as those of the tropics. The ordinary beetles that a chance turn of a stone reveals are like scarabs of gold, turquoise, azurite, bronze, platinum, hurrying and scurrying out of the way. The tarantula-wasp, with his gorgeous orange-colored body and his blue wings, is like a bauble made of precious stones flickering along

The blue and green beetles.

the ground. The great dragon-fly with his many lensed eyes, the bees with black and yellow bodies, the butterflies with bright-hued *Butterflies.* wings, the white and gray millers—all of them dwellers in the sands—are spots of light and color that illumine the desert as the rich jewel the Ethiop's ear. The wings of gauze that bear the ordinary fly upon the air, the feet of ebony that carry the plain black beetle along the rocks, are made with just as much care and skill as the wings of the condor and the foot of the road-runner. Nature in every product of her hand shows the completeness of her workmanship. She made the wings and the legs for a purpose and they fulfil that purpose. They are without flaw and above reproach. Once *Design and character.* more, therefore, have they character and fitness, and once more, therefore, are they beautiful.

I need not now argue beauty in the birds, *Beauty of birds.* the beetles, and the butterflies. You will admit it without argument. The slate-blue of the quail, the gay red of the grosbeak, the charm of the rock-wren, the vivacity of the bobolink or the scale-runner, captivate you and compel your sympathy and admiration. Yes ; but everyone of them is, after his kind, as much of a butcher, just as much of a destroyer, as the wild-cat or the yellow rattlesnake. And they have no more character and perhaps less fitness for the desert life than the sneaking coyote or the flattened lizard which you do not admire. But why are not the coyote and the lizard beautiful too? *Beauty also of reptiles.* Why not the beauty of the horned toad and the serpent? Are we never to love or to admire save where form and color tickle the eye? Are these forever to monopolize the name of beauty and gather to themselves the world's applause?

If we could but rid ourselves of the false ideas, which, taken *en masse*, are called education, we should know that there is nothing ugly under the sun, save that which comes from human *Nature's work all purposeful.* distortion. Nature's work is all of it good, all of it purposeful, all of it wonderful, all of it beautiful. We like or dislike certain things which may be a way of expressing our prejudice or our limitation ; but the work is always perfect of its kind irrespective of human appreciation. We may prefer the sunlight to the starlight, the evening primrose to the bisnaga, the antelope to the mountain-lion, the mocking-bird to the lizard ; but to say that one is good and the other bad, that one is beautiful and the other ugly, is to accuse Nature herself of preference— something which she never knew. She designs for the cactus of the desert as skilfully and as faithfully as for the lily of the garden. Each in its way is suited to its place, and each in its way has its unique beauty of character. And *Precious jewel of the toad.* so, more truly perhaps than Shakespeare himself knew, the toad called ugly and venomous, still holds a precious jewel in its head.

CHAPTER XI

MESAS AND FOOT-HILLS

Flat steps of the desert.

THE word mesa (table), by local usage in Mexico and in the western United States, is applied to any flat tract of ground that lies above an arroyo or valley, as well as to the flat top of a mountain. In a broad, if somewhat strained use of the word, it also means the great table-lands and elevated plains lying between a river-valley and the mountain confines on either side of it. The mesas are the steps **or** benches that lead upward from the river to the mountain, though the resemblance to benches is not always apparent because of the cuttings and washings of intermittent streams, and the breakings and crossings of mountain-spurs.

As you rise up from the Colorado Desert, crossing the river to the east, you meet with a great plain or so-called mesa that extends far across Southern Arizona and Sonora almost up to the Continental Divide. It is broken by

Across Southern Arizona.

194

short ranges of barren mountains, that have the general trend of the main Sierra Madre, and it looks so much like the country to the west of the river that it is usually recognized as a part of the desert, or at the least "desert country."

It is, however, somewhat different from the Bottom of the Bowl or even the valleys of the Mojave. The elevation, for one thing, gives it another character. The rise from bench to bench is very gradual, and to the ordinary observer hardly perceptible; but nevertheless when the foot-hills of the Santa Rita Mountains are reached, the altitude is four thousand feet or more. There is a difference in light, sky, color, air; even some change in the surface of the earth. The fine sands of the lower desert and the sea-bed silts are missing; the mesas lie close up to the mountains and receive the first coarse wash from the sides; the barrancas on the mountain-sides are choked with great masses of fallen rock, with bowlders of granite, with blocks of blackened lava. The arroyos that carry the wash from the mountains—mere ditches and trenches cut through the mesas— are filled with rounded stones, coarse sands, glittering scales of mica, bits of quartz, breaks

Rising up from the desert.

The great mesas.

of agate and carnelian. The mesas themselves are made up of sand and gravel, sometimes long shelvings of horizontal rocks, sometimes patches of terra-cotta, rifts of copper shale, or beds of parti-colored clay.

There is more rain in this upland country and consequently more vegetation than down below. Grease wood grows everywhere and is the principal green thing in sight. So pre-dominant is it that the term "grease wood plains" is not inappropriate to the whole re-gion. Groves of sahuaro stand in the valleys and reach up and over the mountain-tops, chollas and nopals are on the flats; the mes-quite grows in miniature forests. But besides these there are bushes and trees not seen in the basin. Palo fierro, palo blanco, cottonwood live along the dry river-beds, white and black sage on the mesas, white and black oaks in the foot-hills. Then, too, there are patches of pale yellow sun-dried grass covering many acres, great beds of evening primrose, and fields cov-ered with the purple salt-bush. It is quite an-other country when you come to examine it piece by piece.

As you rise higher and higher to the Conti-nental Divide the whole face of the mesa under-

" Grease wood " plains.

Upland vegetation.

goes a further change.   It slips imperceptibly into a grass plain, stretching flat as far as the eye can see, covered with whitened grass, and marked by clumps of yuccas slowly growing into yucca palms.   No rocks, trees, cacti, or grease wood ; no primrose, wild gourd, or verbena.   Nothing but yucca palms, bleached grass, blue sky, and lilac mountains.   It is still in kind a desert country, and it is still called a mesa or table-land ; but its character is changed into something like the great flat lands of Nebraska or the broken plateau country of Montana.

Grass plains.

In the spring, when the snows have melted and the rains have fallen, these plains turn green with young grass and are spattered with great patches of wild-flowers ; but the drouth and heat of early summer soon fade the grasses to a bright yellow, and in the fall the yellow bleaches to a dead white.   There is little wild life left upon these plains.   The bush-birds need more cover than is to be found here, while the ground-birds need more open roadway. In the spring, when the prairie pools are filled with water, there are geese and cranes in abundance ; but they soon pass on north.   These great grass tracts were once the home of count-

Spring and summer on the plains.

less bands of antelope, for it is just such an open country as the antelope loves; but they have passed on, too. In their place roam herds of cattle, and the gray wolf, the coyote, and the buzzard follow the herds.

The grease wood and the grass plains of Arizona and New Mexico are typical of all the flat countries lying up from the deserts; and yet there are many tracts of small acreage in this same region that show distinctly different features. Sometimes there are small beds of flat alkali dust, sometimes beds of soda and gypsum, sometimes beds of salt. Then occasionally there is a broad plain sown broadcast far and wide with blocks of lava—the remnants of a great lava-stream sent forth many centuries ago; and again flat reaches strewn thick with blocks of porphyry that have been washed down from the mountains no one knows just when or how. You are always riding into the unexpected in these barren countries, stumbling upon strange phenomena, seeing strange sights.

And yet as you ascend from the valley of the Colorado moving to the northeast, the lands and the sights become even stranger. For now you are rising to the Great Plateau and the Grand Canyon country—the region of the butte, the vast escarpment, the dome, the cliff, the gorge. It is a more mountainous land than that lying to the south, and it is deeper cut with river-beds and canyons. Yet still you have no trouble in finding even here the flat spaces peculiar to all the desert-bordering territory. There are grease wood plains as at the south and great bare benches that seem endless in their sweep. There are, too, spaces covered with lava-blocks and beds of soda and salt. More rain falls here than at the south or west ; and in certain sections the grass grows rank, the yuccas become trees, and higher up toward Ash Fork the hills are covered with a growth of juniper. Flowers and shrubs are more abundant, birds and animals come and go across your pathway, and there are green valleys with water running upon the surface of the ground. And yet not twenty miles from the green valley you may enter upon the most barren plain imaginable—a place like the Painted Desert, perhaps, where in spots not a living thing of any kind is seen, where there is nothing but dry rock in the mountains and dry dust in the valley. These areas of utter desolation are of frequent enough occurrence in all the regions lying immediately to the north and the east of the Mojave to re-

The Grand Canyon country.

Hills covered with juniper.

The Painted Desert.

mind you that you are still in a desert land, and
that the bench and the arid plain are really a
part of the great waste itself.

Nature never designed more fascinating coun-
Riding on the mesas. try to ride over than these plains and mesas
lying up and back from the desert basin.   You
may be alone without necessarily being lonesome.   And everyone rides here with the feeling that he is the first one that ever broke into
this unknown land, that he is the original dis-
coverer ; and that this new world belongs to
him by right of original exploration and con-
quest.   Life becomes simplified from necessity.
The rever-sion to savagery. It begins all over again, starting at the primitive
stage.   There is a reversion to the savage.   Civ-
ilization, the race, history, philosophy, art—
how very far away and how very useless, even
contemptible, they seem.   What have they to do
with the air and the sunlight and the vastness of
the plateau ! Nature and her gift of buoyant life
are overpowering.   The joy of mere animal existence, the feeling that it is good to be alive
and face to face with Nature's self, drives everything else into the background.

The thin air again. And what air one breathes on these plains—
what wonderful air ! It is exhilarating to the
whole body ; it brightens the senses and sweet-

ens the mind and quiets the nerves. And how clear it is ! Leagues away needle and spine and mountain-ridge still come out clear cut against the sky. Is it the air alone that makes possible such far-away visions, or has the light somewhat to do with it ? What penetrating, all-pervading, wide-spread light ! How silently it falls and how like a great mirror the plain reflects it back to heaven !

Light and air—what means wherewith to conjure up illusions and deceive the senses ! We think we see far away a range of low hills, but, as we ride on, buttes and lomas seem to detach and come toward us. There is no range ahead of us ; there are only scattered groups of hills many miles apart. Far away to the left on a little rise of ground is a wild horse watching us, his head high in air, his nostrils sniffing for our scent upon the breeze. How colossal he seems ! Doubtless he is the last of some upland band, the leader of the troop who through great size and strength was best fitted to survive. But no ; he is only a common little Indian pony distorted to huge proportions by the heated atmosphere. We are riding into the sunset. Ahead of us every notch in the hills, every little valley has a shaft of golden light streaming

The light and its deceptions.

Distorted proportions.

through it.   But turn in your saddle and look
to the east, and the hills we have left behind
us are surrounded by veilings of lilac.   Again
the omnipresent desert air!   We see the

*Changed
colors.*

western hills as through an amber glass, but
looking to the east the glass is changed to pale
amethyst.

How delicately beautiful are the hills that
seem to gather in little groups along the waste!
They are not sharp-edged in their ridges like
the higher mountains.   Wind, rain, and sand
have done their work upon them until there is
hardly a rough feature left to them.   All their
lines are smooth and flow from one into another;
and all the parti-colors of their rocks and soils

*The little
hills.*

are blended into one tone by the light and the
air.   With surfaces that catch and reflect light,
and little depressions that hold shadows, how
very picturesque they are!   Indeed as you
watch them breaking the horizon-line you are
surprised to see how easily they compose into
pictures.   If you tried to put them upon can-

*Painting
the desert.*

vas your surprise would probably be greater to
find how very little you could make of them.
The desert is not more paintable than the Alps.
Both are too big.

These hills—they are usually called lomas—

that one meets with in the plateau region are not of the same make-up as the clay buttes of Wyoming or the gravel hills of New England. They have a core of rock within them and are nothing less than washed-down foot-hills. You will often see a chain of them receding from the range toward the plain, and growing smaller as they recede, until the last one is a mound only a few feet in height. They are flattening down to the level of the plain—sinking into the sandy sea.

Worn-down mountains.

Usually the lomas are seen against a background of dark mountains of which they are or have been at one time a constituent part. For the lomas are the outliers from the foot-hills as the foot-hills from the mountains proper. They are the most worn because they are the lowest down in the valley—in fact the bottom steps which receive not only their own wash but that of all the other steps besides. The mountains pour their waters and loose stones upon the foot-hills, the foot-hills cast them off upon the lomas, and the lomas in turn thrust them upon the plains. But the casting off effort becomes weaker at each step as the sides of the hill become less of a declivity. When the little hill is reached the sand-wash settles about the

The mountain-wash and its effect.

base, and in time the whole mass rises on its
sides and sinks somewhat in the centre, until

Flattening down to the plain.

a mere rise of ground is all that remains. So
perish the hills that we are accustomed to speak
of as "everlasting." It is merely another illustration of Nature's method in the universe.
She is as careless of the individual hill or mountain as of the individual man, animal, or flower.
All are beaten into dust. But the species is
more enduring, better preserved. Year by year
Nature is tearing down, washing down, pulling
to pieces range after range ; but year by year

Mountain-making.

she is also heaving up stupendous mountains
like the Alps, and crackling with a mighty
squeeze the earth's crust into the ridges of the
Rockies and the Andes.

The foot-hills.

The foot-hills are just what their name indi-
cates—the hills that lie at the foot of the mountains. They are not usually detached from the
main range like so many of the lomas, but are a
part of it ; and while not exactly the buttresses
of the mountains, yet they remind one of those
architectural supports of cathedral walls. The
foot-hills themselves are perhaps as firmly supported as the mountains for very often they
stretch down from the mountains in a long
ridge like a spine, and from the spine are

thrown out supporting ribs that trail away into the valleys. In a granite country these foot-hills are usually very smooth, and are made up largely, as regards their surfaces, of the grit and grind of the rocks. The rocks themselves are usually wind worn, rounded by rain and sand, and sometimes fantastic in shape. Often the soft granite wears through in seams and leaves lozenge-like blocks linked together like beads upon a string ; often the whole rock-crown of the hill is honey-combed by the wind until it looks as soft as a sponge. The foot-hills of porphyry are more jagged and rough in every way. The stone is much harder and while it splits like granite and falls along the mountain-side in a talus it does not readily disintegrate. The last bit of it remains a hard kernel, and the porphyry foot-hill is usually a keen-edged mountain in miniature.

Forms of the foot-hills.

The hills have a desert vegetation of grease-wood, cactus, and sage, with occasional trees like the palo verde and the lluvia d'oro ; but their general appearance is not very different from the mesas. Where the altitude is high—say five thousand feet and over—there may be a more radical change in vegetation ; for now the oak begins to appear, and if it is open country

Mountain-plants.

the grasses and flowers show everywhere. Sometimes the foot-hills are covered with a dense chaparral made up of many low trees and bushes; but this growth is more peculiar to the Californian hills west of the Coast Range than to Arizona. Many of the ranges in the Canyon country are almost as bare of vegetation as an ancient lake-bed. And sometimes altitude seems to have little to do with the kinds of growths. Cacti and the salt-bush flourish at six thousand feet as readily as down in the Salton Basin three hundred feet below sea-level. The most dangerous and difficult thing to set up about anything in this desert world is the general law or common rule. The exception—the thing that is perhaps uncommon—comes up at every turn to your undoing.

Bare mountains.

Even the mountains of Arizona that have an elevation of from five to eight thousand feet are often quite bare of timber. The sahuaro, the nopal, the palo verde may grow to their very peaks and still make only a scanty covering. Seen from a distance the southern exposure of the mountain looks perfectly bare; but if you travel around it to the north side where the sunlight does not fall except for a

The southern exposures.

few hours of the day, you will find a growth of bushes, small trees, vines, and grasses that, taken together, form something of a thicket—that is for a desert. And here, too, on the northern exposure you will find the abrupt walls of the *Gray lichens.* peak stained with great fields of orange and gray lichens that lend a color quality to the whole top.

But through the bushes and grasses and lichens the wine-red of the porphyry comes cropping out to tell you that the mountain is a mass of rock, that it holds little or no soil on its sides, that it has not a suspicion of water; and that whatever grows upon it, does so, not by favor of circumstance, but through sheer desert stubbornness. The vegetation is a thin *Still in the desert region.* disguise that is penetrated in a few moments. The arid character of the mountain says plainly enough that we are not yet out of the region of sands and burning winds and fiery sun-shafts. The whole of the Arizona country as far east as the Continental Divide, in spite of its occasional green valleys and few high mountain-ranges with timbered tops, is a slope leading up and out from the desert by gradual if broken steps which we have called mesas or benches. It is a bare, dry land. Its name would imply that the early Spaniards had found it that and called it *arida zona* for cause.*

Yet at times it is a land of heavy cloud-bursts and wash-outs. In the summer months it frequently rains on the mesas in torrents. The bare surface of the country drains this water almost like the roof of a house because there are no grasses or bushes of consequence to check the water and allow it to soak into the ground. The descent from the Divide to the Colorado River is quite steep. The flood of waters rushes down the steps of the mesas and over the bare ground with terrific force. It quickly cuts channels in the low places down which are hurled sand, gravel, and bowlders. The cutting of the channel during the heavy rains is something extraordinary, partly because the stream has great volume and fall, and partly because the channel-bed is usually of soft rock and easily cut. In a few dozen years the arroyo of a mesa that carries off the water from the mountain-range has cut a river-bed many feet deep; in a

Cloud-bursts on the mesas.

The wash of rains.

* The late Dr. Elliot Coues and others reject the obvious *arida zona* of the Spanish in favor of some strained etymologies from the Indian dialects, about which no two of them agree. Why should the name not have come from the Spanish, and why should it not mean just simply arid zone or belt ?

few hundred years the valley-bed changes into a gorge with five hundred feet of sheer rock-wall ; in a few thousand years perhaps the rest-less wearing water of the great river has sunk its bed five thousand feet below the surface and made the Grand Canyon of the Colorado.

Gorge cutting.

The Canyon country is well named, for it has plenty of wash-outs and gorges. Almost any-where among the mountain-ranges you can find them—not Grand Canyons, to be sure, but ones of size sufficient to be impressive without being stupendous. Walls of upright rock several hun-dred feet in height have enough bulk and body about them to impress anyone. The mass is really overpowering. It is but the crust of the earth exposed to view ; but the gorge at Ni-agara and the looming shaft of the Matterhorn are not more. The imagination strains at such magnitude. And all the accessories of the gorge and canyon have a might to them that adds to the general effect. The sheer precipices, the leaning towers, the pinnacles and shafts, the recesses and caves, the huge basins rounded out of rock by the waterfalls are all touched by the majesty of the sublime.

In the canyons.

Upright walls of rock.

And what could be more beautiful than the deep shadow of the canyon ! You may have

had doubts about those colored shadows which
painters of the *plein-air* school talked so much
about a few years ago. You may have thought
that it was all talk and no reality ; but now that
you are in the canyon, and in a shadow, look
about you and see if there is not plenty of color
there, too. The walls are dyed with it, the
stones are stained with it—all sorts of colors
from strata of rock, from clays and slates, from
minerals, from lichens, from mosses. The
stones under your feet have not turned black
or brown because out of the sunlight. If you
were on the upper rim of the canyon looking
down, the whole body of air in shadow would
look blue. And that strange light coming from
above ! You may have had doubts, too, about

the intense luminosity of the blue sky ; but look
up at it along the walls of rock to where it
spreads in a thin strip above the jaws of the
canyon. Did you ever see such light coming
out of the blue before ! See how it flashes from
the long line of tumbling water that pitches over
the rocks ! White as an avalanche, the water
slips through the air down to its basin of stone ;
and white, again, as the snow are the foam and
froth of the pool.

Stones and water in a gorge, wastes of rock

thrust upward into mountains, long vistas of plain and mesa glaring in the sunlight—what things are these for a human being to fall in love with ? Doctor Johnson, who occasionally went into the country to see his friends, but never to see the country, who thought a man demented who enjoyed living out of town ; and who cared for a tree only as firewood or lumber, what would he have had to say about the desert and its confines ? In his classic time, *Desert landscape.* and in all the long time before him, the earth and the beauty thereof remained comparatively unnoticed and unknown. Scott, Byron, Hugo, —not one of the old romanticists ever knew Nature except as in some strained way symbolic *The former knowledge of Nature.* of human happiness or misery. Even when the naturalists of the last half of the nineteenth century took up the study they were impressed at first only with the large and more apparent beauties of the world—the Alps, the Niagaras, the Grand Canyons, the panoramic views from mountain-tops. They never would have tolerated the desert for a moment.

But the Nature-lover of the present, who has taken so kindly to the minor beauties of the world, has perhaps a little wider horizon than his predecessors. Not that his positive knowledge is so much greater, but rather where he lacks in knowledge he declines to condemn.

The Nature-lover of the present.

He knows now that Nature did not give all her energy to the large things and all her weakness to the small things; he knows now that she works by law and labors alike for all; he knows now that back of everything is a purpose, and if he can discover the purpose he cannot choose but admire the product.

That is something of an advance no doubt— a grasp at human limitations at least—but there is no reason to think that it will lead to any lofty heights. Nature never intended that we

Human limitations.

should fully understand. That we have stumbled upon some knowledge of her laws was more accident than design. We have by some strange chance groped our way to the Gate of the Garden, and there we stand, staring through the closed bars, with the wonder of little children. Alas! we shall always grope! And shall we ever cease to wonder?

CHAPTER XII

MOUNTAIN-BARRIERS

THE character of the land lying along the western boundaries of the deserts is very different from that of the Arizona canyon country. Moving toward the Pacific you meet with no mesas of consequence, nor do you traverse many plateaus or foot-hills. The sands extend up to the bases of the Coast Range and then stop short. The mountains rise abruptly from the desert like a barrier or wall. Sometimes they lift vertically for several thousand feet, but more often they present only a steep rough grade. There are cracks in the wall called passes, through which railways lead on to the Pacific ; and there are high divides and saddles —dips in the top of the wall—through which in the old days the Indians trailed from desert to sea, and which are to-day known only to the inquisitive few.

The western mountains.

Saddles and passes.

From the saddles—and better still from the topmost peaks—there are wonderful sights to

be seen. You will never know the vast reach
of the deserts until you see them from a point
of rock ten thousand feet in air. Then you are
standing on the Rim of the Bowl and can see
the yellow ocean of sand within and the blue
ocean of water without. The ascent to that
high point is, however, not easy, especially if
The view from the mountain-top. undertaken from the desert side. But nothing
could be more interesting in quick change and
new surprise than the rise from the hot waste
at the bottom to the cold white-capped peaks of
the top. It is not often that you find mountains with their feet thrust into tropic sands
and their heads thrust into clouds of snow.

Before you start to climb, before you reach
the foot of the mountains, you are struck by
the number of dry washes leading down from
the sides and gradually losing themselves in the
sands. As the eyes trace these arroyos up the
mountain-side they are seen to turn into green
Looking up toward the peak. streaks and finally, near the peak, into white
streaks. You know what that means and yet
can hardly believe that those white lines are
snow-banks packed many feet deep in the canyons ; that from them run streams which
lower down become green lines because of the
grasses, bushes, and trees growing on their

banks; and that finally the streams, after plunging through canyons, fall into the arroyos and are drunk up by the desert sands before they have left the mountain-bases. It seems incredible that a stream should be born; run its course through valley, gorge, and canyon; and then disappear forever in the sands, all within a few miles. Yet not one but many of these mountain-streams have that brief history.

Lost streams.

And at one time they must have been larger, or there were slips of glaciers or avalanches on the mountains; for the arroyos are piled with great blocks of granite and there are rows of bowlders on either side which might have been rolled there by floods or pushed there by an ice-sheet. As you draw nearer, the bowlders crop out in large fields and beds. They surround the rock bases like a deposit rather than a talus, and over them one must pass on his way up the mountain-side.

Avalanches and bowlder-beds.

If you ascend by the bed of the arroyo it is not long before you begin to note the presence of underground water. It is apparent in the green of the vegetation. The grasses are seen growing first in bunches and then in sods, little blue flowers are blooming beside the grasses; alders, willows, and young sycamores

The ascent by the arroyo.

are growing along the banks, and live-oaks are in the stream-bed among the bowlders. As you move up and into the mountain the bed becomes more of a rocky floor, the earth-deposits grow thinner, and presently little water-pockets begin to show themselves.   At first you see them in pot-holes and worn basins in the rock, *Growth of the stream.* then water begins to show in small pools under cut banks, and then perhaps there is a little glassy slip of light over a flat rock in a narrow section of the bed.   Gradually the slip grows in length and joins the pools, until at last you see the stream come to life, as it were, out of the ground.

Rising banks. The banks begin to rise.   As you advance they lift higher and higher, they grow into abrupt walls of rock ; the strata of granite crop out in ragged ledges.   The trees and grasses disappear, and in their place come cold pale flowers growing out of beds of moss, or clinging in rock-niches where all around the gray and orange lichens are weaving tapestries upon the walls.   The bed of the stream seems to have sunken down, but in reality it is rising by steps *Waterfalls.* and falls ever increasing in size.   The stream itself has grown much larger, swifter, more noisy.   You move slowly up and around the falls, each one harder to surmount than the last, until finally you are in the canyon.

The walls are high, the air is damp, the light is dim. The glare and heat of the desert have vanished and in their place is the shadow of the cave. You toil on far up the chasm, creeping *In the gorge.* along ledges and rising by niches, until a great pool, a basin hewn from the rock, is before you; and the hewer is seen waving and flashing in the air a hundred feet as it falls into the pool. Around you and ahead of you is a sheer pitch of rock curved like a horseshoe. It is insurmountable; there is no thoroughfare. You will not gain the peak by way of the canyon. The water-ousel on the basin edge—sole tenant of the gorge—seems to laugh at your ignorance of that fact. Let us turn back and try the ridges.

Up the faces of the spurs and thus by the *The ascent by the ridges.* backbones and saddles to the summit is not easy travelling. At first desert vegetation surrounds you, for the cacti and all their companions creep up the mountain-side as far as possible. The desert does not give up its dominion easily. Bowlders are everywhere, vines and grasses are growing under their shade; and, as you advance, the bushes arise and gradually thicken into brush, and the brush runs into a chaparral. The manzanita, the lavender, and white lilac, the buckthorn, the laurel, the sumac, all throw out stiff dry arms that tear at your clothing. The mountain-covering that from below looked an ankle-deep of grasses and weeds—a velvety carpet only—turns out to be a dense tangle of brush a dozen feet high. It is not an attractive place because the only successful method of locomotion through it is on the hands and knees. That method of moving is peculiar to the bear, and so for that matter

The chaparral.

is the chaparral through which you are tearing your way. It is one of the hiding-places of the

Home of the grizzly.

grizzly. And there are plenty of grizzlies still left in the Sierra Madre. To avoid the chaparral (and also the bear) you would better keep on the sunny side of the spurs where the ground is more open.

You are at the top of one of the outlying spurs

Ridge trails and taluses.

at last and you find there a dim trail made by deer and wolves leading along the ridge, across the saddle, and up to the next spur. As you follow this you presently emerge from the brush and come face to face with a declivity, covered by broken blocks of stone that seem to have been slipping down the mountain-side for cen-

turies. It is an old talus of one of the spurs.
You wind about it diagonally until different
ground is reached, and then you are once more
upon a ridge—higher by a spur than before.

Again the scene changes. An open park-
like country appears covered with tall grass,
the sunlight flickers on the shiny leaves of live- *Among the live-oaks.*
oaks, and dotted here and there are tall yuccas
in bloom—the last of the desert growths to
vanish from the scene. Flowers strange to the
desert are growing in the grass—clumps of yellow violets, little fields of pink alfileria, purple
lilies, purple nightshades, red paint-brushes,
and flaming fire-rods. And there are birds in the *Birds and deer.*
trees that know the desert only as they fly—blue
birds with red breasts as in New England, blue-
jays with their chatter as in Minnesota, blue-
backed woodpeckers with their tapping on dead
limbs as in Pennsylvania. And here was once
the stamping-ground of the mule-deer. Here
in the old days under the shade of the live-oak
he would drowse away the heat of the day and
at night perhaps step down to the desert. He
was safe then in the open country, but to-day
he knows danger and skulks in the depths of
the chaparral, from which a hound can scarcely
drive him.

Onward and upward through the oaks until you are on the top of another ridge. Did you think it was the top because it hid the peak? Ah no; the granite crags are still far above you. And there, yawning at your very feet, is

Yawning canyons.

another canyon whose existence you never suspected. How steep and broad and ragged the walls look to you! And down in the bottom of the canyon—almost a mile down it seems—are huge masses of rock, fallen towers and ledges, great frost-heaved strata lying piled in confusion among trees and vines and heavy

The canyon stream.

brush. Here and there down the canyon's length appear disconnected flashes of silvery light showing where a stream is dashing its way under rocks and through tangled brush down to the sandy sea. And far above you to the right where the canyon heads is a streak of dirty-looking snow. There is nothing for it but to get around the head of the canyon above the snow-streak, for crossing the canyon itself is unprofitable, not to say impossible.

How odd it seems after the sands to see the

Snow.

snow. The long wedge lying in the barranca under the shadowed lee of an enormous spur is not very inviting looking. It has melted down and accumulated dust and dirt until it looks al-

most like a bed of clay. But the little stream
running away from its lowest part is pure ; and
it dashes through the canyon, tumbles into little
pools, and slips over shelving precipices like a
thing of life. Could the canyon have been cut
out of the solid rock by that little stream ? Who
knows ! Besides, the stream is not always so *The wear of
water.*
small. The descent is steep, and bowlders carried down by great floods cut faster than water.

It is dangerous travelling — this crossing of
snow-banks in June. You never know how
soft they may be nor how deep they may drop
you. Better head the snow-bank no matter how
much hard brush and harder stones there may
be to fight against. The pines are above you *The pines.*
and they are beginning to appear near you. Beside you is a solitary shaft of dead timber, its
branches wrenched from it long ago and its
trunk left standing against the winds. And on
the ground about you there are fallen trunks,
crumbled almost to dust, and near them young
pines springing up to take the place of the fallen.
Manzanita and buckthorn and lilac are here,
too ; but the chaparral is not so dense as lower
down. You pass through it easily and press on
upward, still upward, in the cool mountain-air,
until you are above the barranca of snow and un-

der the lee of a vast escarpment. The wall is perpendicular and you have to circle it looking for an exit higher up. For half an hour you move across a talus of granite blocks, and then through a break in the wall you clamber up to the top of the escarpment. You are on a high spur which leads up a pine-clad slope. You are coming nearer your quest.

The pines !—at last the pines ! How gigantic they seem, those trees standing so calm and majestic in their mantles of dark green—how gigantic to eyes grown used to the little palo verde or the scrubby grease wood ! All classes of pines are here—sugar pines, bull pines, white pines, yellow pines — not in dense numbers standing close together as in the woods of Oregon, but scattered here and there with open aisles through which the sunshine falls in broad bars. Many small bushes—berry bushes most of them—are under the pines ; and with them are grasses growing in tufts, flowers growing in beds, and bear-clover growing in fields. Aimless and apparently endless little streams wander everywhere, and ferns and mosses go with them. Bowlder streams they are, for the rounded bowlder is still in evidence—in the stream, on the bank, and under the roots of the pine.

The beautiful mountain-quail loves to scram- *Mountain-quail.*
ble over these stones, especially when they are
in the water; and the mountain-quail is here.
This is his abiding-place, and you are sure to
see him, for he has a curiosity akin to that of
the antelope and must get on a bowlder or a log
to look at you.   And this is the home of hundreds of woodpeckers that seem to spend their
entire lives in pounding holes in the pine-trees
and then pounding acorns into the holes.   It
is a very thrifty practice and provides against
winter consumption, only the squirrels consume
the greater part of the acorns if the blue-jays
do not get ahead of them.   For here lives the
ordinary blue-jay and also his mountain cousin,
the crested jay, with a coat so blue that it might
better be called indigo.   A beautiful bird, but *Indigo jays.*
with a jangling note that rasps the air with discord.   His chief occupation seems to be climbing pine-trees as by the rungs of a ladder.
There are sweeter notes from the warblers, the *Warblers.*
nuthatches, and the chickadees.   But no desert-
bird comes up so high; and as for the common
lawn and field birds like the robin and the
thrush, they do not fancy the pines.

Upward, still upward, under the spreading
arms of the pines! How silent the forest save

for the soughing of the wind through the pine needles and the jangle of the jays! And how thin and clear the mountain-air! How white the sunlight falling upon the moss-covered rocks! It must be that we have risen out of the dust-laden atmosphere of the desert. And out of its heat too. The air feels as though blown to us from snow-banks, and indeed, they are in the gullies lying on either side of us. For now we are coming close to the peak. The bushes have been dwindling away for some time past, and the pines have been growing thinner in body, fewer in number, smaller in size. A dwarf pine begins to show itself—a scraggly tempest-fighting tree, designed by Nature to grow among the bowlders of the higher peaks and to be the first to stop the slides of snow. The hardy grasses fight beside it, and with them is the little snow-bird, fighting for life too.

Upward, still upward, until great spaces begin to show through the trees and the ground flattens and becomes a floor of rock. In the barrancas on the north side the snow still lies in banks, but on the south side, where the sun falls all day, the ground is bare. You are now above the timber line. Nothing shows but wrecked and shattered strata of rock with patches of

The mountain-air.

The dwarf pine.

The summit.

stunted grass. The top is only barren stone. The uppermost peak, which you have perhaps seen from the desert a hundred miles away looking like a sharp spine of granite shot up in the air, turns out to be something more of a dome than a spine—a rounded knob of gray granite which you have no difficulty in ascending.

At last you are on the peak and your first impulse is to look down. But no. Look up! *The look upward at the sky.* You have read and heard many times of the "deep blue sky." It is a stock phrase in narrative and romance; but I venture to doubt if you have ever seen one. It is seen only from high points—from just such a place as you are now standing upon. Therefore look up first of all and see a blue sky that is turning into violet. Were you ten thousand feet higher in the air you would see it darkened to a purple-violet with the stars even at midday shining through it. How beautiful it is in color and how wonderful it is in its vast reach! The dome in- *The dark-blue dome.* stead of contracting as you rise into it, seems to expand. There are no limits to its uttermost edge, no horizon lines to say where it begins. It is not now a cup or cover for the world, but something that reaches to infinity—something in which the world floats.

And do you notice that the sun is no longer *White light.* yellow but white, and that the light that comes from it is cold with just the faintest shade of violet about it ?   The air, too, is changed. Look at the far-away ridges and peaks, some of them snow-capped, but the majority of them bare ; and see the air how blue and purple it looks along the tops and about the slopes. Peak upon peak and chain upon chain disappear to the north and south in a mysterious veil of gray, blue, and purple.   Green pine-clad spurs of the peaks, green slopes of the peaks themselves, keep fading away in blue - green mazes and hazes.   Look down into the canyons, into the shadowed depths where the air lies packed in a *Distant views.* mass, and the top of the mass seems to reflect purple again.   This is a very different air from the glowing mockery that dances in the basin of Death Valley.   It is mountain-air and yet has something of the sea in it.   Even at this height you can feel the sea-breezes moving along *The Pacific.* the western slopes.   For the ocean is near at hand—not a hundred miles away as the crow flies.   From the mountain-top it looks like a flat blue band appended to the lower edge of the sky, and it counts in the landscape only as a strip of color or light.

Between the ocean and the mountain you are standing upon lies the habitable portion of Southern California, spread out like a relief map with its broken ranges, its chaparral-covered foot-hills, and its wide valleys. How fair it looks lying under the westering sun with the shadows drawing in the canyons, and the valleys glowing with the yellow light from fields of ripened barley! And what a contrast to the yellow of the grain are the dark green orchards of oranges and lemons scattered at regular intervals like the squares of a checker-board! And what pretty spots of light and color on the map are the orchards of prunes, apricots, peaches, pears, the patches of velvety alfalfa, the groves of eucalyptus and Monterey cypress, the long waving green lines of cottonwoods and willows that show where run the mountain-streams to the sea!

Southern California.

Yet large as they are, these are only spots. The cultivated portion of the land is but a flower-garden beside the unbroken foot-hills and the untenanted valleys. As you look down upon them the terra-cotta of the granite shows through the chaparral of the hills ; and the sands of the valleys have the glitter of the desert. You know intuitively that all this

The garden in the desert.

country was planned by Nature to be desert. Down to the water-edge of the Pacific she once carried the light, air, and life of the Mojave and the Colorado.

But man has in measure changed the desert conditions by storing the waste waters of the mountains and reclaiming the valleys by irrigation. His success has been phenomenal. Out of the wilderness there have sprung farms, houses, towns, cities with their wealth and luxury. But the cultivated conditions are maintained only at the price of eternal vigilance. Nature is compelled to reap where she has not sown; and at times she seems almost human in the way she rebels and recurs to former conditions. Two, three; yes, at times, four years in succession she gives little rain. A great drouth follows. Then the desert breaks in upon the valley ranches, upon the fields of barley, the orchards of prunes and peaches and apricots. Then abandoned farms are quite as plentiful as in New England; and once abandoned, but a few years elapse before the desert has them for its own. Nature is always driven with difficulty. Out on the Mojave she fights barrenness at every turn; here in Southern California she fights fertility. She is deter-

Reclaiming the valleys.

Fighting fertility.

mined to maintain just so much of desert with just so much of its hardy, stubborn life. When she is pleased to enhance it or abate it she will do so; but in her own good time and way.

Come to the eastern side of the peak and look out once more upon the desert while yet there is time. The afternoon sun is driving its rays through the passes like the sharp-cut shafts of search-lights, and the shadows of the mountains are lengthening in distorted silhouette upon the sands below. Yet still the San Bernardino Range, leading off southeast to the Colorado River, is glittering with sunlight at every peak. You are above it and can see over its crests in any direction. The vast sweep of the Mojave lies to the north; the Colorado with its old sea-bed lies to the south. Far away to the east you can see the faint forms of the Arizona mountains melting and mingling with the sky; and in between lie the long pink rifts of the desert valleys and the lilac tracery of the desert ranges.

The desert from the mountain-top.

The great extent of the desert.

What a wilderness of fateful buffetings! All the elemental forces seem to have turned against it at different times. It has been swept by seas, shattered by earthquakes and volcanoes, beaten by winds and sands, and scorched

The fateful wilderness.

by suns. Yet in spite of all it has endured. It remains a factor in Nature's plan. It maintains its types and out of its desolation it brings forth increase that the species may not perish from the face of the earth.

And yet in the fulness of time Nature designs that this waste and all of earth with it shall perish. Individual, type, and species, all *All shall perish.* shall pass away ; and the globe itself become as desert sand blown hither and yon through space. She cares nothing for the individual man or bird or beast ; can it be thought that she cares any more for the individual world ? She continues the earth-life by the death of the old and the birth of the new ; can it be thought that she deals differently with the planetary and stellar life of the universe ? Whence come the new worlds and their satellites unless from the dust of dead worlds compounded with the energy of nebulæ ? Our outlook is limited indeed, but have we not proof in our own moon *The death of worlds.* that worlds do die ? Is it possible that its bleached body will never be disintegrated, will never dissolve and be resolved again into some new life ? And how came it to die ? What was the element that failed—fire, water, or atmosphere ? Perhaps it was water. Perhaps it died through thousands of years with the slow evaporation of moisture and the slow growth of the—desert.

Is then this great expanse of sand and rock the beginning of the end ? Is that the way our globe shall perish ? Who can say ? Nature plans the life, she plans the death ; it must be that she plans aright. For death may be the culmination of all character ; and life but the process of its development. If so, then not in vain these wastes of sand. The harsh destiny, the life-long struggle which they have imposed upon all the plants and birds and animals have been but as the stepping-stones of character. It is true that Nature taxed her invention to the utmost that each might not wage unequal strife. She gave cunning, artifice, persistence, strength ; she wished that each should endure and fulfil to its appointed time. But it is not the armor that develops the wearer thereof. It is the struggle itself—the hard friction of the fight. Not in the spots of earth where plenty breeds indolence do we meet with the perfected type. It is in the land of adversity, and out of much pain and travail that finally emerges the highest manifestation.

Not in vain these wastes of sand. And this

The desert the beginning of the end?

Development through adversity.

time not because they develop character in desert life, but simply because they are beautiful in themselves and good to look upon whether

*Sublimity
of the waste.*

they be life or death. In sublimity—the superlative degree of beauty—what land can equal the desert with its wide plains, its grim mountains, and its expanding canopy of sky! You shall never see elsewhere as here the dome, the pinnacle, the minaret fretted with golden fire at sunrise and sunset; you shall never see elsewhere as here the sunset valleys swimming in a pink and lilac haze, the great mesas and plateaus fading into blue distance, the gorges and canyons banked full of purple shadow. Never again shall you see such light and air and color; never such opaline mirage, such rosy dawn, such fiery twilight. And wherever you go, by land or by sea, you shall not forget that which you

*Desolation
and silence.*

saw not but rather felt—the desolation and the silence of the desert.

Look out from the mountain's edge once more. A dusk is gathering on the desert's face, and over the eastern horizon the purple shadow of the world is reaching up to the sky. The light is fading out. Plain and mesa are blurring into unknown distances, and mountain-ranges are looming dimly into unknown heights. Warm drifts of lilac-blue are drawn like mists across the valleys ; the yellow sands have shifted into a pallid gray. The glory of the wilderness has gone down with the sun. Mystery—that haunting sense of the unknown—is all that remains. It is time that we should say good-night—perhaps a long good-night—to the desert.

Good-night to the desert.

INDEX

235

OTHER BOOKS IN THE SERIES

ABOUT THE AUTHOR

JOHN C. VAN DYKE was born in 1856 at Green Oaks, a three-peaked mansion still standing on the outskirts of New Brunswick, New Jersey. The son of a bank president who later became a congressman, Van Dyke attended Columbia Law School but never practiced as an attorney. Instead, devoting himself to the aesthetic life, he went on to become the head librarian of the New Brunswick Theological Seminary and held a concurrent appointment as a professor of art history at Rutgers College (now University). His dozens of books on nature, art criticism, and travel won him fame as a foremost culture bearer of the day, earned him the position of art advisor to industrialist Andrew Carnegie, and provided entree into the highest social circles of America and Europe. None of his volumes, however, is as famous or as pivotal as *The Desert*—the first book to praise the desert and alert the nation to its lush heritage of arid sweeps. Van Dyke died in New York City in 1932.

ABOUT THE ESSAYIST

PETER WILD was born in 1940 in Northampton, Massachusetts. A journalist, backpacker, and avid conservationist, he has written and edited over sixty books, both poetry and prose, and was nominated for the Pulitzer Prize in 1973 for *Cochise* (Doubleday), a collection of poetry. In 1997 he edited *Daggett: Life in a Mojave Frontier Town*, a memoir by rancher Dix Van Dyke, for the Johns Hopkins University Press. He is a professor of English at the University of Arizona.

Library of Congress Cataloging-in-Publication Data

Van Dyke, John Charles, 1856–1932.
  The desert : further studies in natural appearances / John C. Van
Dyke ; with a critical introduction by Peter Wild. — Johns Hopkins
pbk ed.
    p.   cm. — (American land classics)
  Originally published: New York : C. Scribner's Sons, 1901.
  Includes index.
  ISBN 0-8018-6224-8 (pbk. : alk. paper)
  1. Southwest, New—Description and travel. 2. Natural history—
Southwest, New. 3. Landscape—Southwest, New. 4. Deserts—Southwest,
New. I. Title. II. Series.
F786.V24   1999
508.315'4'0979—dc21   99-20379
                                                          CIP